Foundations of
Economic Value Added

James L. Grant
Graduate School of Management
Simmons College

Published by  **es**

© 1997 By Frank J. Fabozzi Associates
New Hope, Pennsylvania

This publication is designed to provide accurate and authoritative information in regard to the subject matter covered. It is sold with the understanding that the publisher is not engaged in rendering legal, accounting, or other professional services.

ISBN: 1-883249-24-4

Printed in the United States of America

To Barbara and Our Family

(Erica, Meredith, Hannah, Joel, and Kathryn)

Table of Contents

Preface and Acknowledgments

Advances in the general subject of "economic value added" (EVA)[1] described in this book are in large part the result of a finance journey that dates back to the mid-1970s when I received my graduate training at the University of Chicago Graduate School of Business. At that time, I was deeply immersed in learning about the "modern" financial theories and research of the day, including Eugene Fama's efficient market hypothesis, the portfolio models of Harry Markowitz and William Sharpe, the corporate finance-investment management ideas of Robert Hamada (my dissertation chairman, and now Graduate School of Business Dean), the capital budgeting and capital structure principles of Miller-Modigliani, and the pioneering Black and Scholes option pricing model. That rigorous foundation has in turn given me the insight to recognize the theoretical and large-scale empirical importance of the rapidly emerging EVA measure of corporate profitability.

As a novice first learns about these corporate and investment management developments, it may seem difficult to see the common elements among the various financial models. With experience one realizes that much of finance is concerned with the significance of wealth creation in the context of adding shareholder value. Fortunately, this is where the "just-in-time" EVA metric goes to the head of the finance class since, in principle, this innovative profit measure is the *annualized* equivalent of the firm's net present value (MVA in Stern-Stewart terminology). As an EVA illustration, graduates of corporate finance (who are perhaps now CFOs) will recall that in a well-functioning capital market the firm's operating and investment decisions can be made independently of shareholder "tastes" (or utilities) for present and expected future consumption.

In this rational setting, the favorable net present value — the positive discounted-average EVA — announcements by corporate managers are wealth enhancing for *all* of the firm's existing shareholders, while the investor-perceived negative NPV announcements unfortunately destroy shareholder value. Whether corporate managers realize it or not, this efficient market condition is why they can make investment decisions according to the classic net present value rule.

Likewise, the modern principles of corporate finance reveal that if the capital market is indeed efficient, then these positive average-EVA growth decisions by managers can largely be made without regard to the particular method (debt versus equity) of corporate financing. In effect, the EVA-enhancing decisions by managers in a levered firm (a firm with long-term debt) have the same wealth impact as if the firm were totally unlevered (that is, debt-free). However, with market imperfections corporate managers also need to consider the EVA

---

[1] EVA$^{®}$ is the registered trademark of Stern Stewart & Co. Since this book focuses primarily on the theory and measurement of the firm's real profitability, the more general "EVA" mnemonic is used throughout the book to represent the broader context of this value-added term. That is, "EVA" notation (alone) is used in the chapters to explain both the concept of "economic value added" and its empirical relevance using the commercial EVA$^{®}$ product.

impact of the firm's effective debt-tax subsidy due to the presumably lower weighted average cost of capital.

This corporate finance illustration is just the *beginning* of a systematic understanding of the role of EVA in the theory and practice of finance. If, in principle, MVA is equal to the present value of the firm's anticipated EVA stream, then corporate managers need to see that this MVA and discounted-EVA association is empirically robust in real-time capital markets. However, with some notable exceptions (including a study of mine in the Fall 1996 issue of the *Journal of Portfolio Management*), many of the MVA-EVA discussions to date have been largely based on anecdotal evidence. Moreover, these popular discussions are in all-too-many instances side-lined by secondary questions about the relative information content of the EVA performance metric, as evidenced in the recent "Metric Wars" concerning the financial merits of EVA versus ROE.

As with corporate finance, EVA has many investment implications. For instance, if the firm's capitalization (debt plus equity value) falls short of its EVA-based intrinsic value, then its outstanding bonds and stocks would be undervalued in the marketplace. By purchasing the mispriced securities of firms having, for example, relatively low MVA-to-EVA multiples, the active investor may reap windfall capital gains on a portfolio consisting of the firm's outstanding debt and equity securities. Stock price rises in this investment scenario because the positive EVA announcement increases investors' anticipated residual claim on real future earnings, while bond investors may reap windfall capital gains due to unanticipated credit upgrades on the firm's debt. Hence, investment managers can also see that EVA has joint implications for the valuation of the firm's outstanding debt and equity securities.

In addition to the training I received at the University of Chicago Graduate School of Business, I have received many insights from my professional associates on how to evaluate companies and industries in an investment management context. Research discussions with Wayne Archambo of Boston Partners Asset Management and John Stahr of Fidelity Investments have been invaluable in helping shape my thoughts on the role of EVA in building portfolios of value- and growth-oriented stocks. These company and industry analysis discussions have also been helpful in recognizing that EVA has active investment implications for *both* the firm's outstanding debt and equity securities. In addition, Paul Price, my longtime professional associate at State Street Bank and Trust Company, has again proved to be a significant source of information on investment policy and macroeconomic issues.

On the research side, I am especially grateful to Al Ehrbar — President of the EVA® Institute — and John Allen of Stern Stewart & Co. for their "no-questions-asked" policy of supplying me data on the Performance 1000 Universe. For the record, my enthusiasm about EVA (and its present value equivalent, MVA) as an innovative tool for measuring real corporate profits has in no way been influenced by anyone at Stern-Stewart. I would also like to thank my daughter, Meredith Grant, for quantitative research assistance, especially in constructing the exhibits used in the key EVA chapters on company and industry analysis.

A special word of thanks goes to Frank Fabozzi at Frank J. Fabozzi Associates. His encouragement and flexibility has indeed made it a real pleasure to take this MVA-EVA step forward. It was Frank, not I, who had the insight to expand upon my study in the Fall 1996 *Journal of Portfolio Management*. Finally, I owe a great deal of gratitude to Deans Margaret Hennig and Anne Jardim of the Simmons Graduate School of Management in Boston for their positive reinforcement and the time out to achieve this hopefully positive "surplus return" on human capital.

James L. Grant

Chapter 1

The EVA Revolution

In a market-driven economy many companies will create wealth. Other firms, however, will undoubtedly destroy it. Discovering those economic factors that lead to wealth creation and destruction among companies is important to many constituencies, not the least of which is corporate officials and investment managers. For corporate managers, wealth creation is fundamental to the economic survival of the firm. Managers that fail (or refuse) to see the importance of this financial imperative in an open economy do so at the peril of the organization and their own careers.

Finding the "best" companies and industries in the marketplace is of prime importance to investment managers. With the proper financial tools, portfolio managers may be able to enhance their active performance over-and-above the returns available on similar risk-indexed passive strategies. This wealth-discovery and company-selection process is now being assisted by a new analytical tool called EVA. The innovative changes that this financial metric has spawned in the twin areas of corporate finance and investment management are the driving force behind what can be termed the "EVA Revolution."

ECONOMIC VALUE ADDED (EVA)

The analytical tool called EVA, for Economic Value Added, was commercially developed during the 1980s by the corporate advisory team of G. Bennett Stewart III and Joel Stern.[1] This financial metric gained early acceptance from the corporate financial community because of its innovative way of looking at a firm's real profitability. Unlike traditional measures of corporate profitability — such as net operating profit after tax (NOPAT) and net income — EVA looks at the firm's "residual profitability," net of both the direct cost of debt capital and the *indirect* cost of equity capital. In this way, EVA serves as a modern measure of corporate financial success because it is closely aligned with the shareholder wealth-maximization requirement.

Large firms like AT&T, Coca Cola, and Quaker Oats, as well as EVA-newcomers such as Eli Lilly, are using this measure as a guide to creating "economic value added" for their shareholders. Bonuses and incentive pay schemes at these U.S. firms have been built around the manager's ability (or lack thereof) to generate

---

[1] EVA® is a registered trademark of Stern Stewart & Co. This financial metric is rapidly becoming the practitioner's tool for measuring the firm's real "economic value added." Stewart-Stern refers to the present value equivalent of this profit measure as the firm's market value added (MVA).

For an insightful discussion of the commercial EVA® product, along with many applications of how this profit metric can be used in a corporate finance setting, see G. Bennett Stewart III, *The Quest for Value* (HarperCollins, New York: 1991).

positive EVA within the firm's operating divisions. Positive payments may accrue to managers having divisional after-tax operating profits that on balance exceed the relevant "cost of capital," while negative incentive payments may occur if the longer-term divisional profits fall short of the overall capital costs. Thus, by accounting for the cost of both debt *and* equity capital, EVA gives managers the incentive to act like shareholders when making corporate investment decisions.

EVA is now gaining rapid popularity in the investment community. The June 1996 Conference on "Economic Value Added" at CS First Boston is testimony to this exciting financial development. Indeed, global equity research and stock valuation at this major investment banking firm are now based on the innovative EVA technology. Other large firms are taking a serious look, and Merrill Lynch is now using this metric to evaluate its managers in the corporate and institutional banking sector. The EVA metric is also making some meaningful inroads in the world of global performance analytics. Moreover, the recently-published empirical study by the author of this book in the Fall 1996 issue of the *Journal of Portfolio Management* shows that EVA is now being advanced in both the academic and financial communities.[2]

DEFINITIONS OF EVA

From an accounting perspective, EVA can be defined as the difference between the firm's net operating profit after tax (NOPAT) and its weighted-average *dollar* cost of capital. As a result, EVA differs from traditional accounting measures of aggregate corporate profitability including, earnings before interest and taxes (EBIT), EBIT plus depreciation (EBITD), net income, and even NOPAT because it fully accounts for the firm's overall capital costs. This analytical difference is important to the firm's owners since the EVA metric is — net of both the direct cost of debt capital and the *indirect cost* of equity capital — as reflected in the shareholders' required return on the firm's risky stock. In this context, EVA can be expressed in more general terms as:

$$EVA = NOPAT - \$ \text{ Cost of Capital}$$

In this expression, the firm's *dollar* cost of capital is calculated by multiplying the *percentage* cost of capital times the capital investment according to:

$$\$ \text{ Cost of Capital} = [\% \text{ Cost of Capital}/100] \times \text{Investment}$$

Likewise, the percentage cost of capital is obtained by taking a "weighted average" of the firm's after-tax cost of debt and equity capital as shown by:

$$\% \text{ Cost of Capital} = [\text{Debt Weight} \times \% \text{ After-Tax Debt Cost} \\ + \text{ Equity Weight} \times \% \text{ Cost of Equity}]$$

---

[2] See James L. Grant, "Foundations of EVA for Investment Managers," *Journal of Portfolio Management* (Fall 1996).

Exhibit 1: NSF Corporation

Time Period	Investment ($ millions)	EVA ($ Millions)
0 (now)	100.0	0.0
1	0.0	15.0
Weighted Average Cost of Capital (COC) = 10%		

The Present Value Interpretation

EVA can also be defined in terms of the firm's "market value added." In this context, MVA is equal to the *present value* of the firm's expected future EVA. Additionally, since MVA is equal to the market value of the firm less the total "book capital" employed in the business, it appears that EVA is related to the *intrinsic value* of the firm and its outstanding debt and equity securities. Stating these concepts in more formal terms yields the Stern-Stewart expression between the firm's "market value added (MVA)" and its "economic value added (EVA)":

MVA = Firm Value – Total Capital

MVA = [Debt plus Equity Value] – Total Capital

MVA = PV of Expected Future EVA

These financial definitions have important implications for the firm's owners. Companies having positive EVA momentum should on balance see their stock (and perhaps, bond) prices go up over time as the increasing profits net of the overall capital costs lead to a rise in the firm's "market value added." In contrast, firms with returns on invested capital that fall short of the weighted-average cost of capital should see share price decline as the adverse EVA outlook lowers the intrinsic (present) value of the firm.

Hence, by incorporating EVA analysis into the company evaluation process, securities analysts may enhance the overall pricing accuracy of their research recommendations. Also, with EVA corporate managers have an innovative financial tool for assessing whether or not their *planned* investment in real assets will lead to wealth creation for the shareholders.

MVA and EVA: A Simple Present Value Example

As a basic illustration of the present value relationship between the firm's MVA and EVA, consider a two-period example where NSF's (for, "New Start-up Firm") investment and financing opportunities are like those listed in Exhibit 1. The exhibit indicates that if NSF invests $100 million today in real assets, then it can expect to create $15 million of positive EVA in the future period.

With a "discount rate" or cost of capital at 10%, the "net present value" of NSF's investment opportunity is $13.64 million:

$$NPV = MVA$$
$$= \$EVA(1)/(1 + COC)$$
$$= \$15/(1.1) = \$13.64 \text{ million}$$

The $13.64 million in "market value added (MVA)" shows that NSF is a wealth creator. By adding this positive NPV figure to NSF's initial capital investment of $100 million, one obtains the market value of the firm, at $113.64 million:

$$V = \text{Initial Investment} + MVA$$
$$= \$100 + 13.64 = \$113.64 \text{ million}$$

Moreover, if one makes the convenient assumption that NSF's capital investment is financed with 100% debt, then the aggregate equity capitalization for the firm is the $13.64 million in market value-added (MVA). With 1 million shares of stock outstanding, each share is then worth $13.64 ($13.64 million/1 million shares) in market value terms. Thus, in this "two-period" example, the firm's aggregate MVA is equal to the present value of its expected future "economic value added (EVA)."

MVA AND EVA: GROWTH CONSIDERATIONS

The EVA and MVA linkage can also be extended to a multi-period framework. In this context, the author develops a simple "constant growth" model to show the pricing importance of both the firm's near-term EVA outlook and its long-term EVA growth rate in determining overall corporate valuation.[3] In this "Gordon-like" model, the relationship between the firm's MVA and its EVA-outlook for the future is expressed as:

$$MVA = EVA(1)/(COC - g)$$

where, EVA(1) is the firm's current EVA outlook (one-year ahead forecast), g is the firm's assessed long-term EVA growth rate, and COC is the familiar weighted-average cost of debt *and* equity capital.

This constant-growth EVA model shows that the firm's market value added (MVA) is positively related to its near-term EVA outlook, as measured by EVA(1), as well as the firm's assessed long-term EVA growth rate, g. As shown, the firm's MVA is also negatively related to any unanticipated changes in its overall weighted-average cost of (debt and equity) capital, COC. However, in view of modern capital structure principles, this "cost of capital" interpretation does not imply that the firm's corporate debt policy has any meaningful impact on the valuation of the firm and its outstanding debt and equity shares.[4]

---

[3] Grant, "Foundations of EVA for Investment Managers."

[4] Peter Bernstein eloquently captures the essence of the "M&M (Miller-Modigliani)" capital structure principles when he states that "the cost of capital depends far more on the quality of corporate earning power than on the structure of paper [debt and equity] claims." For Bernstein's insightful comment on corporate debt policy, see Peter L. Bernstein, "Pride and Modesty," *Journal of Portfolio Management* (Winter 1991).

Exhibit 2: Market Value-Added: Major Wealth Creators

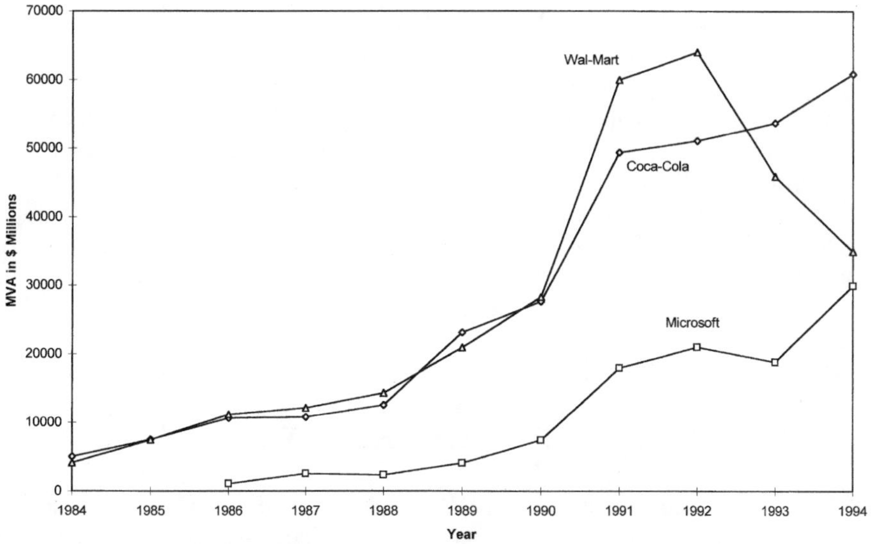

PREVIEW OF WEALTH CREATORS

Let's now look at the MVA and EVA relationship for some major wealth creators and wealth destroyers. The MVA and EVA characteristics for Coca-Cola, Microsoft Corporation, and Wal-Mart Stores are shown in the wealth-creator illustrations in Exhibits 2 and 3. These U.S. large firms were among the top ten wealth creators (based on MVA rankings) in the "1995 Performance 1000 Universe" collected by Stern Stewart & Co.

Exhibit 2 shows that wealth creators like Coca-Cola, Microsoft, and Wal-Mart Stores have substantially positive MVAs that grow rapidly over time. At year-end 1994, Coca-Cola's total net present value was $60.85 billion while Microsoft and Wal-Mart were reporting MVA values of $29.9 and $35 billion, respectively. During the 8-year period from (year-end) 1986 to 1994, Microsoft's net present value was growing at a compound yearly rate of nearly 52%. For the 10-year period ending at year-end 1994, Coca-Cola's MVA was growing at an annualized rate of 28.2%, while Wal-Mart was reporting a respectable overall average growth rate of about 23.7% — although Wal-Mart's growth in net present value in the 8-year period ending in 1992 was noticeably higher, at 40.7%.

Exhibit 3 shows the economic source of the positive net present value being generated by the three U.S. wealth-creating firms. Specifically, this exhibit suggests that Coca-Cola, Microsoft, and Wal-Mart have positive MVAs because their EVAs are both positive and generally growing at an exceptional rate over time. At $1.88 billion, Coca-Cola's 1994 EVA is not only positive, but this financial metric grew by 28.79% in the 10-year period after 1984. With MVA and EVA growth rates at 28% during this decade, the two exhibits indicate that Coke's net present value closely "tracked" the firm's ever-rising "economic value added." Likewise, Microsoft's 8-year EVA growth rate of 59% seems to have provided the necessary fuel for its abnormal MVA growth rate, of 52%.

On balance, it appears that Wal-Mart's MVA growth rate of 23.7% is consistent with its 10-year EVA growth rate of about 22%. However, the major decline (nearly $30 billion) in this firm's MVA (Exhibit 2) during 1993 and 1994 suggests that investors were exceedingly optimistic about Wal-Mart's ability to generate EVA for the future. On the other hand, the MVA and EVA experiences of Coca-Cola and Microsoft in the two years after 1992 (Exhibits 2 and 3, jointly) suggest that investors may have incorrectly gauged the EVA-producing abilities of these powerful wealth creators.

PREVIEW OF WEALTH DESTROYERS

Exhibits 4 and 5 show the EVA and MVA relationships for three U.S. firms that — ironically enough — became large wealth destroyers in recent times. Specifically, these exhibits report the MVA and EVA experiences of IBM, General Motors, and RJR Nabisco Holdings, Inc. for the recent decade covering (year-end) 1984 to 1994. These firms were listed among the bottom ten firms — based on MVA rankings — in the 1995 survey by Stern-Stewart.

Exhibit 3: Economic Value-Added: Major Wealth Creators

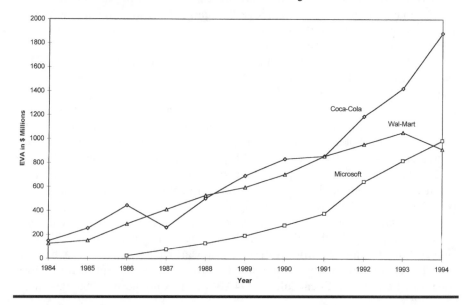

Exhibit 4: Market Value-Added: Major Wealth Destroyers

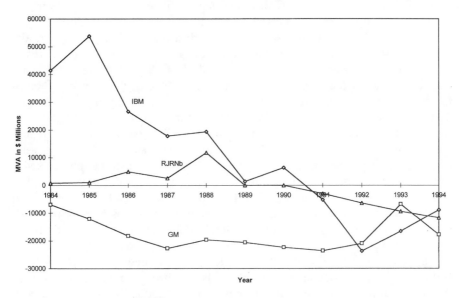

Exhibit 5: Economic Value-Added: Major Wealth Destroyers

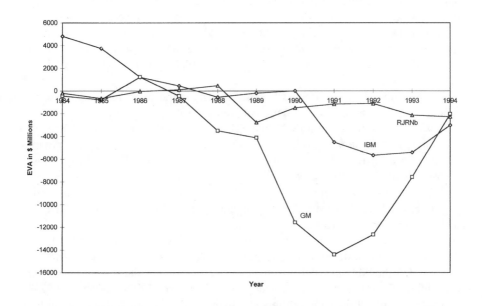

Exhibit 4 shows that the net present value figures for the three U.S. wealth destroyers are strikingly different than the reported MVA values for the "New Guard" of modern capitalism — including, firms like Coca-Cola, General Electric (not shown), Microsoft, and Wal-Mart Stores. Indeed, this wealth destroyer exhibit shows that IBM alone wasted some $50 billion in net present value in the 10-year period ending at year-end 1994. IBM's "market value added (MVA)" dropped from $41.49 billion at year-end 1984 to about −8.86 billion by the end of 1994. Moreover, Exhibit 4 also shows that this large U.S. firm destroyed some $65.2 billion of MVA in the 8-year period ending in 1992.

This exhibit shows that General Motor's MVA experience in the reporting decade was rather dismal too. This recent wealth waster had eleven full years of negative net present value during 1984 to 1994. GM's market value added at year-end 1984 was −$6.9 billion, while its total net present value at year end 1994 was down to about −17.8 billion. In effect, the market value for this automaker was consistently below the "book capital" employed in the business for the entire decade. This also means that General Motor's "price-to-book value" ratio was consistently below unity in the 1984 to 1994 reporting period.

Exhibit 4 also reveals some troublesome MVA findings for RJR Nabisco Holdings, Inc. In particular, it seems that this firm became a wealth destroyer in the aftermath of the largest hostile takeover in U.S. history. In this context, RJR Nabisco's MVA was positive in the 5-year period 1984 to 1988, and then turned negative in the 4-year reporting interval after 1990. A closer look at the financial happenings at this firm might reveal that RJR's MVA declined during this period because of two unwelcome "company events" — the hostile acquisition by Kohlberg, Kravis, and Roberts and the financial fallout from the public's anti-smoking campaigns. Whatever the cause, the negative MVA values reported for this wealth destroyer ranged from −$3 billion in 1991, down to −11.76 billion at year-end 1994.

Exhibit 5 shows the EVA experiences for the three recent U.S. wealth wasters. As expected, the economic source of the negative net present value for IBM, General Motors, and RJR Nabisco (Exhibit 4) is their EVA experiences that ultimately turned negative over time. For instance, IBM was posting a positive EVA of $4.82 billion at year-end 1984. By year-end 1992, this large wealth destroyer's EVA had declined to −5.67 billion. Meanwhile, IBM's net present value (MVA, in Exhibit 4) dropped by some $65 billion during this 8-year reporting period. Since 1992, however, the MVA experience for IBM suggests that investors feel that the firm's negative EVA experiences may have finally "bottomed out."

Exhibit 5 also shows that from 1986 to 1991 General Motors posted a dramatic decline in its economic value added. At year-end 1991, this automobile firm's real profitability *net* of the overall capital costs had declined to −$14.42 billion. Coinciding with this negative EVA figure is GM's adverse MVA value of −$23.57 billion for year-end 1991. Although this automaker's EVA improved considerably in the three years after 1991, the volatility revealed in its MVA values (Exhibit 4) during this period suggests that investors — whether correctly or incorrectly — still lacked confidence in GM's fundamental ability to generate "economic value added" for the future.

Finally, RJR Nabisco's MVA experiences in the 1984 to 1994 period also seem consistent with its EVA behavior. In particular, the firm's MVA and EVA figures were largely increasing up to the hostile acquisition. Then, however, RJR Nabisco's market value added and its economic value added were consistently negative in the post-1990 years. By the end of 1994, the twin MVA and EVA measures of corporate financial success (or, failure) for this large firm were at –$11.76 billion (MVA) and –$2.27 billion, respectively.

NEW EVA HORIZONS

Before delving too deeply into the conceptual and empirical side of EVA, it is important to spell-out what this book *is* and is *not* designed to do. First, this book examines both the conceptual and large-scale empirical role (or lack thereof) of EVA in determining the "franchise value" of the firm. In this context, an attempt will be made to assess the empirical role of EVA in the cross-section of U.S. corporations and industries, along with the information content of this financial metric for firms and the economy over time.

Since EVA is fundamentally-related to the market value of the firm, the results of this new empirical horizon represent potentially valuable information for corporate managers and investors alike. By undertaking this broad research effort, it is hoped that this book will elevate the innovative EVA metric — thereby, lifting it above the current realm of anecdotal evidence that is all too often cited in the conventional EVA discussions — to a larger conceptual and empirical position in financial economics where it truly belongs.[5]

This book also explores new EVA horizons by showing how to use this metric in valuing companies and industries. In this context, the research shows how to use published financial reports — such as the forward-looking company reports from Value Line — to estimate the firm's anticipated future EVA, and, in turn, its current MVA. These valuation procedures can be used by corporate managers and investors to assess whether the firm's outstanding securities are valued correctly in the marketplace.

Additionally, quantitative techniques are used to find the most attractive industries or sectors in the capital market for active investing. Regression analyses and the Markowitz portfolio model are used to assess the most attractive EVA opportunities in the marketplace. The text also develops a two-factor EVA model — based on the positioning of the economy-wide return on capital (ROC) and the average cost of capital (COC) — to explore some meaningful financial happen-

---

[5] For an interesting popular discussion of EVA (with only anecdotal substance), see Shawn Tully, "The Real Key to Creating Wealth," *Fortune* (September 20, 1993).

ings at the macro-economic level. The EVA findings at both the industrial and economic level are truly exciting, and await the investigation of the reader.

On the other hand, it is important to mention that this book is *not* meant to demonstrate that EVA is the only measure of corporate profitability that should be used by managers and investors in determining the market value of the firm and its outstanding shares. Given the present state of empirical "infancy" that EVA research is at, the author does not find it instructive to engage in the popular "Metric Wars" (ROE versus EVA, for example) that seem to detract from recognizing the importance of this financial measure. Suffice it to say that EVA is a "top down" approach to looking at the firm's real profitability in a way that is intrinsically-linked to its overall net present value. At the very least, therefore, the reader should find that the EVA research described here offers new insights that are consistent with the general principles of wealth maximization.

Finally, it should be mentioned that Stern-Stewart should be credited for their efforts in commercializing an innovative measure of corporate profits — that, in practice, can serve as the financial analyst's tool for estimating the firm's real "economic value-added." Having said that, it is also important to recognize that they are not the only individuals in finance or accounting to develop a practitioner approach to estimating the firm's profits *net* of the overall capital costs.

For instance, Robert Anthony of Harvard University is known in the managerial accounting field for his early efforts in adjusting corporate profits for the associated capital costs. Additionally, published research during the 1970s by Alfred Rappaport is consistent with estimating the firm's weighted average cost of capital in a (CAPM) way that is consistent with the commercial EVA product.[6] Moreover, in the theory of finance, EVA is one of many *equivalent* ways of estimating the market value of the firm and its outstanding shares.

SUMMARY

The financial motivation for taking notice of the "EVA revolution" should now be "crystal clear." In a prospective sense, this analytical tool suggests that companies that are experiencing positive EVA momentum should see their stock prices go up over time, as the increasing profitability *net* of the overall capital costs leads to a rise in the market value of the firm. In contrast, firms having negative EVA reports should see a noticeable decline in their equity values as the adverse real profits lead to a fall in the firm's net present value. EVA changes are also likely to

---

[6] I am indebted to Frank Fabozzi of Yale University for pointing out that some of the early managerial accounting work on adjusting profits for the cost of debt and equity capital should be attributed to Robert Anthony of Harvard University.

That Rappaport recognized the economic importance of adjusting corporate profits by a capitalization rate that reflects the overall cost of financing can be found in, Alfred Rappaport, "Strategic Analysis for More Profitable Acquisitions," *Harvard Business Review* (July/August 1979).

impact, either positively or negatively, the firm's credit rating, and therefore the valuation of its risky bonds. Discovering these financial happenings before they occur is at the heart of the EVA Revolution.

Chapter 2 looks at the role of EVA in financial theory. Here it will be demonstrated that EVA is positive when the firm's after-tax return on invested capital is greater than its overall cost of capital. In this context, the firm creates market value added (MVA) by investing in projects having a positive "net present value." When EVA is negative, however, the firm's managers destroy wealth by investing in capital projects having after tax returns that fall short of the weighted average cost of debt and equity capital. In the next chapter, some recently published research will also be presented to show the empirical relationship between the MVA and EVA measures for U.S. large capitalization firms.

Chapter 2

EVA in the Theory of Finance

MVA is often defined as the present value of the firm's expected future EVA. The economic foundation for this insightful present value interpretation lies in the neoclassical wealth model developed by Irving Fisher during the early 1930s. In recent times, the major tenets of the neoclassical model were used by University of Chicago Professors Eugene Fama and Merton Miller in their book, *The Theory of Finance*, as the theoretical basis for illustrating the modern principles of corporate finance.[1]

These financial principles include the importance of "net present value" analysis in determining the market value of the firm and the powerful dividend and capital structure "irrelevance principles" of modern corporation finance. Indeed, Merton Miller of the University of Chicago shared — along with William Sharpe and Harry Markowitz for their pioneering investment works — in the 1990 Nobel Prize in Economic Sciences for his innovative insights into these corporate financial matters.[2]

The neoclassical wealth model can be used in a fundamental sense to show the powerful role of EVA in the wealth creation process. The neoclassical model is presented in this chapter to demonstrate the conceptual importance of this financial metric in three meaningful valuation cases: (A) the case of wealth creation, (B) the case of wealth destruction, and (C) the role of EVA in the event of wealth neutrality. Alternatively, the financial illustrations show the wealth impact of positive, negative, and zero economic value added (EVA). The next chapter focuses on how to estimate EVA, while Chapters 4 and 5 report some large-scale empirical evidence for recent wealth creators and wealth wasters.

---

[1] Irving Fisher's pioneering economic research is described in Irving Fisher, *The Theory of Investment* (New York: Augustus M. Kelley, Publishers, 1965; Reprinted from the original 1930 edition). The modern financial insights of Professors Fama and Miller can be found in Eugene F. Fama and Merton H. Miller, *The Theory of Finance* (New York: Holt, Rinehart, and Winston, 1972).

It may be instructive to note that in *The Quest for Value*, Stewart correctly references the 1961 Modigliani-Miller paper on dividend policy and corporate valuation as a theoretical basis for EVA. (See Merton H. Miller and Franco Modigliani, "Dividend Policy, Growth, and the Valuation of Shares," *Journal of Business* (October 1961).) Since NPV (and therefore, MVA) analysis rests on its own financial merits, without any reference to corporate dividend (or debt) policy, I prefer to emphasize Fisher's neoclassical wealth model as the real source of EVA.

This earlier recognition is not meant to detract in any way from the pricing significance of the Modigliani-Miller paper. Indeed, their models on corporate valuation are used at a later point in this book.

[2] Markowitz and Sharpe shared in the 1990 Nobel Prize in Economic Sciences for their creative work in portfolio theory. Sharpe's Capital Asset Pricing Model (CAPM) serves as the basis for estimating the cost of equity in the conventional EVA model.

Exhibit 1: NSF's Investment Opportunity: Positive Economic Value-Added

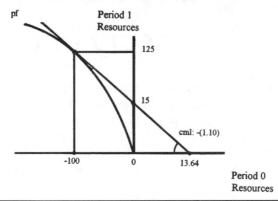

TENETS OF THE NEOCLASSICAL WEALTH MODEL

The theoretical importance of positive EVA can be illustrated by taking a closer look at the present value example presented in Chapter 1. Suppose again that NSF (for New Start-Up Firm) has the opportunity to borrow and invest $100 million in real assets at time period 0 (now). The firm's managers expect that this investment will generate a one-time cash flow of $125 million in the future (period 1). Exhibit 1 illustrates the expected cash flow and wealth implications of NSF's investment opportunity.

NSF's investment-opportunity set is represented by the curve labeled *pf*, for production frontier. By investing $100 million today, the curve shows that the firm can expect to generate $125 million in the future period. In Exhibit 1, the "gross present value" of NSF's investment opportunity is found by dividing the expected future cash flow, CF(1), by the slope of the "capital market line," (1+COC). With a cost of capital (COC) at 10%, the gross present value of NSF's investment decision is therefore $113.64 ($125/ 1.1) million. The assessed gross present value figure represents the overall market value of the firm at time period 0.

The "net present value" of NSF's investment opportunity can now be determined in the conventional way. At $13.64 million, the "market value added" for NSF's initial shareholders is obtained by subtracting the firm's total investment cost, $100 million, from the $113.64 million in estimated gross present value:

$$NPV(0) = MVA(0)$$
$$= GPV(0) - \text{Investment Cost}$$
$$= \$125/(1.1) - 100$$
$$= \$113.64 - \$100 = \$13.64 \text{ million}$$

Thus, Exhibit 1 shows that by efficiently using their productive-investment ideas, the managers (founders) of NSF have increased the market value of the firm's initial shares from *zero* to the current maximum level of $13.64 million.

CASE A: WEALTH CREATION WITH POSITIVE EVA

Nothing has been said up to this point about the *direct* role of EVA in the wealth creation process. However, a closer inspection of the classic NPV model (Exhibit 1) shows that NSF's "market value added (MVA)" can be expressed in another informative way. Specifically, NSF's net present value can also be viewed as the present value equivalent of the firm's expected future EVA. This financial result occurs because EVA is the "residual (or surplus) income" which is left after subtracting the total dollar cost of capital from the firm's expected cash flow.

NSF's expected future EVA is the $15 million figure that was given in the present value illustration in Chapter 1. The economic content of this figure is now revealed in Exhibit 1 by subtracting the future capital costs, $110 million ($100 x 1.1), from the expected cash flow generated by the firm's current investment opportunity. At $13.64 million, NSF's market value added (MVA) is then determined by dividing the expected residual income (EVA), $15 million, by the slope of the capital market line, (1.1):

$$NPV(0) = MVA \text{ (Market Value Added)}$$
$$= \$EVA(1)/(1 + COC)$$
$$= \$15/ (1.1) = \$13.64 \text{ million}$$

In this application of the neoclassical wealth model, MVA is equal to the present value of the firm's expected future EVA. With positive anticipated economic value added for the future, the two-period illustration shows that NSF is in fact a "wealth creator" in the current period.

Moreover, it should be apparent that NSF's expected EVA — and therefore, its current MVA — is positive only if the firm's managers invest in real assets having an after-tax rate of return on capital (ROC) which exceeds the overall cost of capital (COC). At 15%, this favorable "residual return on capital" (ROC-COC) is the underlying economic source of NSF's $13.64 million in market value added:

$$NPV(0) = \$EVA(1)/(1 + COC)$$
$$= \$I[ROC\text{-}COC]/(1 + COC)$$
$$= \$100 [0.25 - 0.1]/(1.1)$$
$$= \$13.64 \text{ million}$$

This financial result occurs because the firm's expected EVA in the two-period wealth model is equal to the initial capital investment *times* the anticipated residual (surplus) rate of return on invested capital, (ROC-COC).

ROC and COC: Microsoft Corporation

Consider Microsoft Corporation as a powerful example of the financial importance of having a positive "residual rate of return" on capital. In this context, Exhibit 2 shows the after-tax rate of return on capital (ROC) versus the cost of capital (COC) for this computer software services company during the 1986 to 1994 period.

Exhibit 2: Microsoft: Return on Capital versus Cost of Capital

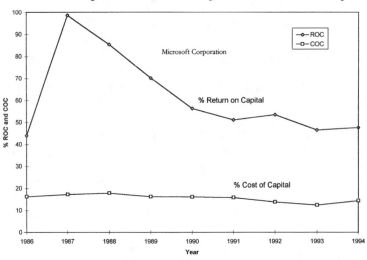

As revealed in Chapter 1, Microsoft had a large positive MVA because its EVA was both positive and growing at an exceptional rate over time. In Exhibit 2 it is possible to see that the firm's large positive EVA (and therefore, MVA) is due to its exceptionally positive residual return on capital — whereby the after-tax rate of return on invested capital is greater than the cost of capital (*equity* cost, in Microsoft's case) by a substantial margin.

Exhibit 2 shows that Microsoft's after-tax capital return varied from 44.11% in 1986, to a high of 98.73% in 1987, and then back to 47.56% in 1994. For the 9-year reporting period, the computer software services company had an outstanding average return on capital, at 61.5%. Meanwhile, Microsoft's cost of capital ranged from a high of 17.88% in 1988 to a comparably lower rate of 12.37% at year-end 1993. The firm's average cost of (equity) capital was 15.61% for the 9-year reporting period shown in the exhibit.

Taken together, the capital return and capital cost findings for Microsoft indicate that the "residual return on capital" was substantially positive for the overall reporting period. Exhibit 2 also reveals that the volatility in this technology firm's residual capital return (and therefore, its EVA and MVA) is primarily due to variations in the after-tax return on capital (ROC). The cost of capital factor (COC) for Microsoft was relatively stable during the 9-year reporting period.

The empirical findings for Microsoft are illustrative of the "residual return on capital" role in the wealth creation process. The company graphs presented in Chapter 1 and this chapter suggest that firms having positive EVA do so because their after-tax return on invested capital exceeds the weighted average cost of capital. In turn, the positive EVA announcement is clearly "good news" to shareholders as it leads to a sizable increase in the firm's market value added.

This favorable NPV (MVA, in Stern-Stewart jargon) result is one of the major predictions that evolves from the neoclassical wealth model.

CASE B: WEALTH DESTRUCTION WITH NEGATIVE EVA

The neoclassical wealth model can also be used to gain insight on the financial characteristics of wealth destroyers. For example, suppose that NSF's managers expect that the $100 million investment today will generate an after-tax cash flow of, say, $107.50 million in the future period. The wealth consequence of the firm's 7.5% ($107.50/100) return on capital in view of the 10% capital cost is shown in Exhibit 3.

The exhibit shows that if NSF invests $100 million today, it then expects to generate a cash flow of $107.50 at period 1. Upon subtracting the future capital costs, at $110 million, from the company's expected future cash flow, the investor sees that the firm is left with a negative residual income of −$2.5 million. This negative $2.5 million figure is NSF's expected "economic value added (EVA)" in the reduced operating performance (that is, ROC set at 7.5%) environment.

If NSF is a wealth destroyer in the future (due to the negative anticipated EVA), then it must also be a wealth waster in the present. By discounting the negative anticipated EVA by the 10% cost of capital, one obtains the adverse net present value result:

$$
\begin{aligned}
NPV(0) &= MVA(0) \\
&= EVA(1)/(1 + COC) \\
&= -\$2.50/1.1 \\
&= -\$2.27 \text{ million}
\end{aligned}
$$

Exhibit 3: NSF's Investment Opportunity: Negative Economic Value-Added

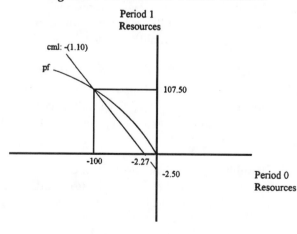

Exhibit 4: IBM: Return on Capital versus Cost of Capital

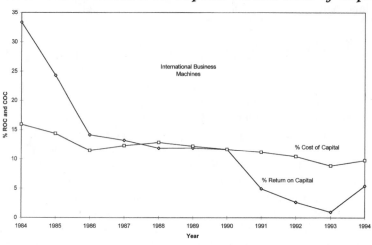

As a perceived wealth destroyer, it should also be apparent that NSF's MVA is negative because the after-tax return on capital falls short of the anticipated capital costs. In this context, the net present value of −$2.27 million can also be calculated by multiplying the firm's "residual (or surplus) return on capital," at −2.5%, by the initial capital investment of $100 million:

$$NPV(0) = MVA(0)$$
$$= \$I[ROC\text{-}COC]/(1 + COC)$$
$$= \$100 \ [0.075 - 0.1]/(1.1)$$
$$= -\$2.27 \ million$$

Thus, NSF's negative MVA is due to its poor EVA outlook. The adverse EVA forecast is in turn caused by the negative assessed residual capital return (ROC– COC) of −2.5%. With these figures, NSF's managers (founders) would not be able to attract the necessary investment capital to start up their new business.

ROC and COC: IBM Corporation

On a more practical level, a fascinating illustration of a recent wealth waster is IBM. Exhibit 4 shows the well-known computer firm's after-tax return on capital (ROC) versus the cost of capital (COC) during the 1984 to 1994 period. The exhibit shows that IBM's post-tax return on capital fell precipitously during the recent reporting decade.

At 33.4%, Exhibit 4 shows that IBM had an exceptional after-tax return on capital for 1984. However, by year-end 1988, the firm's after-tax capital return had fallen to 11.86%, and then remained around this level up to year-end 1990. During these years, IBM experienced a dramatic decline in its "residual return on capital," as reflected in the narrowing gap between the firm's after-tax capital return and the cost of capital. Indeed, IBM's surplus (residual) return on capital declined from 17.5% (33.4%–15.9%) at year-end 1984 to about *zero* percent during the 1988 to 1990 period.

Meanwhile, the computer giant's EVA dropped from $4.8 billion in 1984 to just $3 million by year-end 1990. During these dismal years, IBM lost some $35 billion in market value added (MVA). Exhibit 4 shows that things got even worse for IBM investors in the post-1990 period when the after-tax return on capital (ROC) fell below the weighted average cost of capital, COC. By year-end 1992 the large computer firm had destroyed another $30 billion in net present value. Although IBM's financial condition improved during 1993 and 1994, the firm still had a sizable negative MVA figure of –$8.86 billion at year-end 1994.

The empirical findings for IBM are suggestive of the financial dangers that result when a firm's after-tax capital returns fall short of the capital costs. With a positive after-tax return on capital for each year during the 1984 to 1994 reporting period, it would seem that the firm was still making money — albeit, a smaller amount when measured relative to invested capital each year. However, the evidence reveals that IBM was in fact a major wealth destroyer during this period. The declining "residual return on capital" for IBM — that eventually turned negative in the post-1990 years — was the economic source of the firm's negative market value-added.

CASE C: WEALTH NEUTRALITY WITH ZERO EVA

Finally, the neoclassical wealth model can also be used to assess the financial consequences of *zero*-expected EVA. If, for example, NSF's assessed after-tax return on capital is 10%, then the firm's expected future EVA is zero. This results because the expected future cash flow from the firm's initial investment decision is the same as the anticipated capital costs, at $110 million. In this instance, the firm's aggregate net present value must be zero:

$$\begin{aligned} NPV(0) &= MVA(0) \\ &= \$I[ROC - COC]/(1 + COC) \\ &= \$100 \, [0.1 - 0.1]/(1.1) \\ &= 0.0 \end{aligned}$$

If NSF has *zero*-expected EVA in the future (and therefore, *zero*-MVA today), the firm's aggregate market value is the same as the initial capital investment, $100 million. In the 10% (ROC=COC) investment environment the firm's residual return on capital is zero, and its market-value to book-capital ratio is unity.

Moreover, if NSF has some initial period 0 resources, then the current shareholders would be just as well off if the corporate managers pay the funds out as a dividend payment on the firm's stock. In the event of market imperfections —

perhaps due to differential dividend and capital-gains taxation — the firm's shareholders might be better off if the firm's managers were to repurchase the firm's outstanding common stock. In principle, though, the stock repurchase program is a *zero*-MVA, or wealth-neutral investment activity.

Corporate actions that result in wealth-neutrality should be taken seriously by the firm's managers when they do not have any positive EVA-generating opportunities for the future. Although these programs do not create any new wealth for the shareholders, they do not destroy it either. In contrast, managerial actions (or, inactions) that result in wealth losses to the shareholders like those experienced by General Motors, IBM, and RJR Nabisco Holdings during the past decade were financially unconscionable, especially when the wealth-preserving financial alternatives were available.

EVA AND CORPORATE VALUATION: THE CONSTANT GROWTH MODEL

Here's a numerical illustration of the linkage between MVA and EVA in a multi-period setting. Because of varying assumptions about the firm's investment opportunities, there are many different ways to express the formal linkage between the firm's expected EVA and its corporate valuation. A simple multiperiod approach is obtained by assuming that the firm's expected EVA is growing at some constant rate of growth (g) each year, forever. With this simplifying assumption, the firm's market value-added can be expressed as:[3]

$$MVA = EVA(1)/(COC - g)$$

where EVA(1) is the firm's current EVA outlook, g is the expected long-term EVA growth rate, and COC is the overall cost of capital. This "Gordon-like" model only makes sense for firms having a cost of capital that on average exceeds the long-term EVA growth rate, g. Otherwise, the firm's investment opportunities have to be separated into multiple stages of economic growth Some important variable-growth approaches to corporate valuation using the EVA measure are covered in a later chapter.

The "constant growth" model indicates that if NSF's EVA growth rate is zero, then the market value added (MVA) from the current investment opportunity is equal to $150 ($15/0.1) million. If the firm's managers can engage in investment activities that increase the long-term EVA growth rate to, say, 2.5%, then NSF's market value added would rise to $200 million.

$$MVA = \$15/(0.1 - 0.025)$$
$$= \$200 \text{ million}$$

---

[3] See James L. Grant, "Foundations of EVA for Investment Managers," *Journal of Portfolio Management* (Fall 1996).

Exhibit 5: Regression Statistics for Performance 1000 Universe at Year-End 1993

MVA/Capital = 1.80 + 17.14 EVA/Capital
(t-value)　　(16.30)　(21.34)

Adjusted R^2 = 31.6%
N = 983 Firms

In this instance, the 2.5% EVA growth rate has increased NSF's "intrinsic" value by some $50 million. In turn, the firm's total present value rises from $250 million with the zero-growth assumption to $300 million in the 2.5% model. Thus, NSF's managers have a clear wealth incentive to make investment decisions that enhance the firm's ability to generate EVA, both now and in the future.

MVA AND EVA: SOME LARGE-SCALE EMPIRICAL EVIDENCE

The empirical connection between MVA and EVA can be examined in a more general context by analyzing the financial data collected by Stern-Stewart. In particular, they report EVA®-related information for the 1000 largest capitalization U.S. stocks. Some of the more pertinent financial data listed in the Performance Universe include:

• Market Value Added (MVA)
• Economic Value Added (EVA)
• Total Capital (Debt plus Equity)
• Rate of Return on Capital % (ROC)
• Cost of Capital % (COC)

where EVA equals the firm's net operating profit after tax (NOPAT) less the dollar cost of capital. MVA is defined as the market value of the firm (debt and equity capitalization) less the total "book capital" employed in the business. As demonstrated in this chapter, the firm's market value added (MVA) is also equal to the present value of the expected future EVA.

Exhibit 5 shows the statistical relationship between the MVA-to-Capital (dependent variable) and EVA-to-Capital (explanatory variable) ratios that was estimated in the recent Grant study for year-end 1993.[4] The exhibit reveals that a statistically significant relationship exists between the two measures of corporate financial success. With a slope coefficient of 17.14, and a t-statistic of 21.34, the EVA-to-Capital ratio is a highly significant financial variable.

---

[4] Grant, "Foundations of EVA for Investment Managers."

Exhibit 6: Multiple Regression Statistics for Performance 1000 Universe at Year-End 1993

MVA/Capital = −1.86 + 0.338 COC + 0.172 [ROC−COC]
  (t-value)   (−3.85) (7.74)   (22.09)

Adjusted R^2 = 37.4%
N = 983 Firms

Indeed, it is helpful to point out that an explanatory variable — like the EVA/Capital ratio — is generally considered to be statistically significant when the t-statistic exceeds (the absolute value of the number) *two*. The regression statistics in Exhibit 5 also reveal that 31.6% (adjusted R^2) of the movement in the MVA-to-Capital ratios for U.S. large capitalization firms at year-end 1993 is explained by the *cross-sectional* variation in the EVA-to Capital factor.

In addition, Exhibit 6 reveals the source of the positive relationship between the EVA and MVA variables in the Performance 1000 Universe at year-end 1993. This exhibit looks at the statistical importance of movements in both the cost of capital, COC, and the residual return on capital, (ROC-COC), factors on corporate financial success. The exhibit shows that the size of the difference between a company's after-tax rate of return on capital, ROC, and the cost of capital, COC, has a significant impact on the firm's fundamental ability to generate "economic value added" for shareholders.

With a slope of 0.17, and a t-statistic of 22, the residual return on capital (ROC less COC) has a significant impact on the MVA-to-Capital ratios for the large U.S. firms listed in the Performance Universe. Taken together, the empirical findings presented in Exhibits 5 and 6 suggest that "good firms" do in fact have favorable stock (and possibly bond) prices because their post-tax rate of return on invested capital (ROC) is more than sufficient to cover the overall capital costs.

It is also interesting to see that the cost of capital factor (COC) shown in Exhibit 6 has a significant positive impact on the firm's market value added. With a slope of 0.34, and a t-statistic of 7.74, the cost of capital seems helpful in understanding the cross-sectional variation in the MVA-to-Capital ratios for the U.S. large capitalization firms. This finding may be due in part to an underlying positive relationship between the firm's cost of capital, COC, and its after-tax capital return, ROC — whereby high return, but also more volatile, firms and industries (like technology, for example) have a relatively high required rate of return.

SUMMARY

This chapter uses the neoclassical wealth model to show that MVA is equal to the present value of the firm's expected EVA. As Fama and Miller point out in their pioneering book, *The Theory of Finance*, the NPV model is based on the assumption of a perfectly competitive capital market. The capital market is said to be perfect when (1) there are no tax or transaction cost differentials, (2) investors can freely enter and exit the capital market without restriction, (3) investors have equal access to all relevant information, and (4) investors prefer more expected wealth to less. With these competitive conditions, the portfolio investment decisions of any individual — and the corporate financing actions of the firm — have no effect whatsoever on the established market rate of interest.

One of the major benefits of an efficient capital market is that firms can make investment decisions based on the NPV (or, in popular terms, MVA) rule. By investing in real assets having an after-tax capital return that exceeds the overall capital cost, corporate managers enhance the wealth of *all* of the firm's current shareholders, regardless of their individual preferences for consumption today versus expected consumption in the future. Moreover, in a competitive capital market, investors can borrow and lend at the same (risk-adjusted) rate of interest to effect their desired consumption patterns over the life-cycle.

Since imperfections surely exist in "real world" capital markets, the relevant question for both investors and corporate managers alike is whether the predictions of the NPV (and therefore, EVA) model are consistent with the empirical evidence. As revealed throughout the various chapters in this book (especially Chapters 4 and 5) the answer to this question seems to be a resounding yes. Wealth creators have positive EVA because their after-tax return on invested capital exceeds the overall cost of capital. In turn, the empirical evidence clearly shows that wealth destroyers lose market value added (MVA) because their post-tax capital returns fall short of the weighted average cost of debt and equity capital. These powerful research findings also shed positive light on the field of financial economics in general.

Chapter 3

How to Measure EVA

Estimating EVA in practice can be a challenging exercise for investors and corporate managers alike because of two key measurement issues. In order to estimate EVA, the financial analyst often needs to recast the firm's (pro-forma) income statement in a way that shows the after-tax operating profit that is available to *all* of the firm's owners — including both the debt and equity securityholders. Second, and more importantly, the analyst needs to recognize that the accountant's standard measure of "profit" is an incomplete measure of economic income.[1]

This measurement problem happens because traditional accounting measures of profitability — like EBIT and EBITD on a pre-tax basis, and net operating profit after taxes (NOPAT) and net income in a post-tax situation — do not account for the firm's cost of equity capital. As a result, they do not reflect the investor's required rate of return for assuming both business and financial risk.

Moreover, this accounting omission is important when viewed in a corporate valuation context. By focusing research efforts on measures such as net income and even NOPAT, corporate managers may mistakenly believe that the firm *should be* creating wealth for the shareholders. However, an in-depth EVA analysis may reveal that shareholder wealth is actually falling in the marketplace because the positive accounting profit is not sufficient to cover the firm's overall capital costs. In economic terms, these costs include both the direct cost of debt capital and the *indirect* cost of equity capital. Moreover, since EVA emphasizes the firm's "residual income," this measurement problem cannot be resolved with a mere "repackaging" of the firm's accounting statements.

LEVERED AND UNLEVERED FIRMS

Some helpful insight on how to estimate EVA is obtained with knowledge of what Fama and Miller refer to as the "levered firm."[2] They show that in a world of taxes *and* deductibility of debt interest expense, that the market value of the levered

---

[1] This chapter is *not* meant to serve as a substitute for the Stern-Stewart approach to estimating EVA. The chapter employs an "unlevered cash flow" approach to estimating EVA, while highlighting the key capital market issues — such as the beta controversy and the potential irrelevance of corporate debt policy — that should be considered when estimating EVA.

For an extensive treatment of the accounting complexities that may arise when calculating EVA, see G. Bennett Stewart III, *The Quest for Value* (Harper Collins, New York: 1991).

[2] See Eugene F. Fama and Merton H. Miller, *The Theory of Finance* (New York: Holt, Rinehart, and Winston, 1972).

firm (a firm with debt outstanding) is equal to the present value of the equivalent business-risk "unlevered firm" plus the market value of the levered firm's interest tax shield from corporate debt financing:

$$V_L = V_U + tD$$

In this valuation expression, the V-notation refers to the market value of the levered and unlevered firms, respectively, while the term tD represents the present value of the levered firm's expected annual interest tax subsidy.

In principle, the levered firm derives its market value from the present value of three economic sources: (1) the unlevered firm's operating cash flows that are generated by the investment in real assets, (2) the annual depreciation tax shield that is available to the equivalent business-risk unlevered firm, and (3) the yearly interest tax shield that is available to the shareholders of the levered firm, that, by definition, finances its growth opportunities with both long-term debt and equity financing.

Measuring EVA: A Numerical Illustration

As a practical example of how these profit sources factor into the EVA calculation, suppose that NSF has grown substantially over time, and is now called SLF-for Successful Levered Firm. The income statement and relevant balance sheet information for SLF are presented in Exhibit 1.[3]

This exhibit shows the basic revenue and expense items that might appear on a typical income statement for a manufacturing firm. The accounting statement could be examined in many traditional ways. For instance, SLF reports $360 million in net profit after tax on a revenue base of $3400 million. The firm's net profit margin is 10.6%, while its gross profit margin is 41.2% (1,400/3,400). Likewise, SLF's Earnings Per Share and its "Cash EPS" were $1.80 and $2.80, respectively, on the 200 million shares outstanding. Also, the return on equity (ROE) for SLF's stockholders was 15% (360/2,400).

Estimating EVA for SLF

Although SLF's financial statements can be examined in many traditional ways, the primary focus here is to see how they can be used to assess the firm's economic value added. As introduced in Chapter 1, EVA is defined as the difference between the firm's net operating profit after tax (NOPAT) and the overall cost of capital expressed in dollar terms. Armed with some new terminology pertaining to levered and unlevered firms, the two-step EVA calculation can now be shown more clearly as:

---

[3] It should be mentioned that this EVA discussion takes a slightly different approach to dealing with depreciation in comparison with the Stern-Stewart approach. Specifically, EBITD is used as the firm's pre-tax operating cash flow rather than EBIT. This allows for a *direct* focus on the two different tax subsidies — in the form of the unlevered firm's depreciation tax subsidy and the levered firm's interest tax subsidy — received by the unlevered and levered firms. It is also assumed that the "General and Administrative Expenses" account on the simple income statement has a *maintenance* account that sufficiently covers asset obsolescence.

Exhibit 1: SLF
Income Statement and Selected Balance Sheet Information

	Year-End: in $millions	
Sales		$3,400
Less: CGS		2,000
Gross Profit		$1,400
Less:		
Selling Expense	$160	
Gen. and Adm. Exp.	300	
EBITD	$940	
Depreciation (Dp)	200	
EBIT		$740
Less: Interest Expense		$140
Net Profit Before Tax		$600
Less: Taxes (rate=40%)		$240
Net Profit after Tax		$360

EPS = 360/200 = $1.80

Cash EPS   = EPS + (Dp/200)
                    = 1.80 + (200/200)
                    = 2.80

Balance Sheet Information for SLF:*
Long Term Debt = 1200 (1/3 of Capital)
Stockholders Equity = 2400 (2/3 of Capital)

Total Capital = 3600

* Beginning of Year

$$EVA = UNOPAT - \$COC$$

where UNOPAT is the *unlevered* portion of SLF's (cash) operating profit after tax that is attributed to the firm's product sales and cash operating expenses — *net* of any unlevered taxes due. In turn, the COC term is the familiar weighted average cost of debt and equity capital from modern corporation finance.

The EBITD term on SLF's income statement is important in the estimation of its unlevered net operating profit after tax (UNOPAT). In particular, this income statement item is essential because it provides the analyst with an estimate of the pre-tax operating cash flow that is being generated by SLF when viewed as an *unlevered* firm. To be sure, SLF's EBITD is higher up on the income statement as it reflects the pre-tax operating cash flow that is available to all of the firm's outstanding securityholders. Moreover, investor uncertainty about this pre-tax cash flow measure is a direct reflection of the business risk that is inherent in the ongoing firm.

Exhibit 2: SLF
Calculation of the Unlevered Net Operating Profit After Tax
(Step A: UNOPAT)

$$\begin{aligned}
\text{UNOPAT} &= \text{EBITD} - \text{Taxes} \\
&= \text{EBITD} - t\,[\text{EBITD} - \text{Depreciation}] \\
&= \text{EBITD}\,(1 - t) + \text{Depreciation Shield} \\
&= \text{EBITD}\,(1 - t) + t\,D_p \\
&= 940\,(1 - 0.4) + 0.4 \times 200 \\
&= 564 + 80 \\
\text{UNOPAT} &= \$644 \text{ million}
\end{aligned}$$

In a world of corporate taxes, with deductibility of depreciation expense, SLF's unlevered after-tax operating cash flow can be estimated from two economic sources. These profit sources include the firm's pre-tax operating cash flow (EBITD), and SLF's annual depreciation tax subsidy, tDp. This unlevered operating cash flow calculation is shown in Exhibit 2. In this illustration, the term, UNOPAT, is used to represent SLF's unlevered net operating (cash) profit after tax.

At $644 million, SLF's net operating profit after tax (UNOPAT) is calculated by subtracting the firm's unlevered taxes from the pre-tax operating profit, EBITD. In Exhibit 2, it is important to note that SLF's depreciation expense, $200 million, has no direct bearing on the firm's after tax operating cash flow since, in principle, this accounting-based expense is a non-cash outlay.[4] However, SLF's depreciation expense has an indirect impact on SLF's net operating profit after tax through the depreciation tax shield, tDp. With deductibility, SLF's unlevered corporate taxes are $80 million lower than they would be in the absence of the depreciation write-off. Moreover, because of time value of money considerations, this depreciation tax subsidy could be used to show the possible EVA benefits of using accelerated depreciation methods in enhancing the firm's market value.

SLF's Cost of Capital

Exhibit 3 illustrates how to estimate the dollar cost of capital for SLF. In this exhibit, the firm's cost of capital (COC) is estimated by taking a weighted average of the after-tax cost of the debt and equity capital using the *target* debt weight, w_d, in SLF's levered capital structure.

SLF's overall cost of capital (COC) can be "rolled up" in the following way. The first step involves the calculation of the firm's after-tax cost of debt. In this context, SLF's pre-tax debt cost can be estimated with knowledge of the interest expense item on the income statement, and the "book debt" figure on the balance sheet. With this information, the firm's pre-tax cost of debt is:

---

[4] Fama and Miller, *The Theory of Finance*.

Exhibit 3: SLF
Calculation of the $ Cost of Capital (Step B: $COC)

% Cost of Capital = debt weight × after-tax cost of debt
+ equity weight × cost of equity
$= w_d ×$ [Pre-tax Debt Cost $× (1 - t)$]
$+ w_e ×$ Cost of Equity
$= 1/3 × [(140/1200) × (1 - 0.4)] + 2/3 × 0.15$ *
$= 1/3 × [0.117 (0.6)] + 2/3 × 0.15$
$= 1/3 × [0.07] + 0.10$
$= 0.123$, or 12.3%

* CAPM Cost of Equity at 15%: R_f% + MRP% *times* Beta: 7% + 6% × 1.33

Pre-tax debt cost = $Interest/LT Debt
= 140/1200
= 0.117, or 11.7%

SLF's after-tax cost of debt is then obtained by tax adjusting the 11.7% pre-tax debt cost by the (assumed) corporate tax rate of 40%:

After-tax debt cost = Pre-tax Debt Cost $× (1 - t)$
= 0.117 (1 - 0.4)
= 0.07, or 7%

Thus, SLF borrows money on the average at 11.7%, and receives an interest tax subsidy from the government (taxpayers) of 4.68%.

Estimating the Cost of Equity

Next, the cost of capital formula (Exhibit 3) requires an estimate of the cost of equity capital. This major component of the firm's weighted average cost of capital can be estimated in many ways. However, one modern approach to estimating the firm's equity cost is obtained by using the Capital Asset Pricing Model (CAPM) developed by William F. Sharpe (and others) during the mid-1960s.[5] In this asset pricing model, the firm's equity cost is calculated by adding a business and financial risk premium to the "riskless" rate of interest, R_f. The total equity risk premium is determined in a CAPM context by multiplying an estimate of the economy-wide "Market Risk Premium (MRP)" by the expected relative risk (beta) of the company's stock:

Cost of Equity = R_f + MRP × Beta

---

[5] See William F. Sharpe, "Capital Asset Prices: A Theory of Market Equilibrium under Conditions of Risk," *Journal of Finance* (September 1964).

With CAPM, three easily-obtained inputs can be combined to estimate the cost of equity capital. If, for example, the treasury bond yield is 7%, the assessed market risk premium is 6%, and the (levered) equity beta is 1.33, then SLF's cost of equity capital is:

$$\text{Cost of Equity} = 0.07 + 0.06 \times 1.33$$
$$= 0.15, \text{ or } 15\%$$

The 15% expected cost of equity is a measure of the return that shareholders require for assuming *both* the business (operating) and financial (due to the debt) risk of the ongoing firm.

Another look at Exhibit 3 reveals that SLF's cost of capital is 12.3%. This capitalization rate for the firm is calculated by taking a weighted average of the 7% after-tax cost of debt and the 15% expected cost of the equity. With this development, it is now a simple matter to calculate SLF's *dollar* cost of capital. In particular, the dollar-capital cost is obtained by multiplying the 12.3% cost of capital figure by the estimated "book capital" employed in the business:

$$\$ \text{ Cost of Capital} = [\% \text{ Cost of Cap./100}] \times \text{ Total Capital}$$
$$= [12.3/100] \times \$3600$$
$$= \$442.80$$

Combining the EVA Inputs

Taken together, Exhibits 2 and 3 show how to estimate the two major EVA drivers — the *unlevered* net operating profit after tax (UNOPAT) and the dollar cost of capital ($COC). The basic income statement and balance sheet provided some necessary, yet incomplete information for EVA calculation. On the positive side, these traditional accounting statements were helpful in estimating SLF's unlevered net operating profit (UNOPAT, in Exhibit 2) and the firm's after-tax cost of debt (shown in Exhibit 3). However, the income statement and the balance sheet failed to provide any information regarding the shareholder's required rate of return for assuming the firm's operating (business) and financial risk. Discovering the wealth implications of this accounting omission is the heart of the EVA Revolution.

Exhibit 4 reveals that Successful Levered Firm (SLF) is in fact a wealth-creating firm. In this context, the firm's "residual income" is $201.20 million. This favorable surplus happens because SLF's unlevered net operating profit after tax, $644 million, exceeds the overall capital costs, $442.80. If this positive EVA consideration is expected for the future, then the classic NPV model suggests that SLF would be a "wealth creator" in the current period.

In addition, Exhibit 4 shows that the economic source of NSF's positive EVA is its favorable "residual return on capital." At 5.6%, this surplus spread results from netting out the 12.3% cost of capital from the attractive 17.9% after-tax return on capital. Of course, the same 5.6% surplus (residual) rate of return results when dividing the $201.20 in estimated positive EVA by the total "book capital (at $3,600 million)" employed in the business.

Exhibit 4: SLF Corporation
Economic Value Added (Step A - Step B)

$$\text{EVA} = \text{UNOPAT} - \$ \text{ Cost of Capital}$$
$$= 644 - 442.80$$
$$= \$201.20*$$

SLF is a Wealth Creator!

*SLF is a wealth creator because it has a positive "Residual Return on Capital" (RROC) where:

$$\text{RROC} = \text{ROC} - \text{COC}$$
$$= [644/3600] - [442.80/3600]$$
$$= 0.179 - 0.123$$
$$= \text{EVA/Capital}$$
$$= 201.2/3600$$
$$\text{RROC} = 0.056 \text{ or } 5.6\%$$

A Closer Look at the Levered and Unlevered Firm

The EVA definition that is frequently mentioned in the financial press is helpful in convincing the reader of the importance of this innovative metric. Yet at the same time, the oft-cited definition of EVA belies the complexity of the actual calculation. For instance, in a 1993 Fortune Magazine article, *"The Real Key to Creating Wealth,"* the author states that "EVA is simply after-tax operating profit, a widely used measure, minus the total annual cost of capital."[6] This popular EVA definition is simple enough. However, difficulties can arise when trying to implement the *seemingly* basic concept in practice.

For example, look again at SLF's income statement shown in Exhibit 1. To the unsuspecting, it would seem that SLF's after tax operating profit could be calculated by subtracting the firm's taxes, at $240 million, from the Earnings Before Interest and Taxes (EBIT). This simplistic approach to calculating after-tax operating profit could in turn bias EVA downward because of the $200 million in *non-cash* depreciation expense — although if not recognized elsewhere, some financial charge is necessary for economic obsolescence.

Unfortunately, EVA estimation problems do not disappear when EBIT is replaced by EBITD. This is due to the fact that SLF's $240 million tax figure is already net of the $56 million tax subsidy (0.4 × $140 million) that it receives as a *levered* firm. Failure to properly recognize the economic source of the levered firm's overall tax shields would incorrectly bias EVA upward. For SLF, this EVA-bias happens because the $56 million annual interest tax shield is already accounted for in the calculation of the firm's dollar weighted average cost of capital (Exhibit 3).

The above discussion brings to light the benefit of looking at EVA in the context of the *unlevered* firm's net operating profit after-tax (UNOPAT). In partic-

---

[6] See Shawn Tully, "The Real Key to Creating Wealth," *Fortune* (September 20, 1993).

ular, Exhibit 5 shows a comparison between the after-tax operating cash flows generated by SLF as a levered and unlevered firm, respectively.

At $700 million, Exhibit 5 shows that the levered net operating profit after-tax (LNOPAT) figure is higher than that of SLF as an equivalent business-risk unlevered firm. The difference between the two post-tax cash flow measures is in effect the interest tax subsidy received by the levered firm. At $56 million, this operating cash flow differential is estimated by multiplying SLF's assumed tax rate, at 0.4, times the $140 million interest expense on the firm's long term debt.

However, EVA is already impacted in a beneficial way by the subtraction of the $56 million interest tax shield from the after-tax dollar cost of capital (Exhibit 3). In effect, deductibility of the interest expense for SLF has lowered the firm's 11.7% pre-tax cost of debt down to 7%. Thus, the (unweighted) percentage tax benefit to the firm's cost of capital is 4.7%:

$$\text{Debt-Related Benefit in } \% \text{ COC} = t \, [\text{Interest/Debt}]$$
$$= 0.4 \, [140/1200]$$
$$= 0.4 \, [0.117]$$
$$= 0.047, \text{ or } 4.7\%$$

Expressing this finding in dollar terms reveals the $56 million benefit that is already reflected in SLF's after-tax dollar cost of capital:

Exhibit 5: SLF
Levered and Unlevered Operating Cash Flows

Levered Net Operating Profit After Tax (LNOPAT):

$$\begin{aligned}
\text{LNOPAT} \quad &= \text{EBITD} - \text{Taxes} \\
&= \text{EBITD} - t \, [\text{EBITD} - Dp - \text{I}] \\
&= [\text{EBITD} \, (1 - t) + t \, Dp] + t \, \text{I} \\
&= \text{UNOPAT*} + \text{Interest Shield} \\
&= 644 + 0.4 \, [140] \\
&= \$700 \text{ million}
\end{aligned}$$

* Unlevered Net Operating Profit After Tax:

$$\begin{aligned}
\text{UNOPAT} \quad &= \text{EBITD} - \text{Taxes} \\
&= \text{EBITD} - t \, [\text{EBITD} - Dp] \\
&= [\text{EBITD} \, (1 - t) + t \, Dp] \\
&= \$644 \text{ million}
\end{aligned}$$

$$\begin{aligned}
\text{Difference} \quad &= \text{LNOPAT} - \text{UNOPAT} \\
&= t \; \textit{times} \; \text{Interest Expense} \\
&= \text{Interest Shield} \\
&= \$56 \text{ million}
\end{aligned}$$

$$\text{Debt-Related Benefit in } \$ \text{ COC} = 0.047 \times \text{Debt}$$
$$= 0.047 \times 1200$$
$$= \$56 \text{ million}$$

Thus, using the levered firm's after-tax operating profit (LNOPAT) instead of the unlevered cash flow (UNOPAT) would therefore bias EVA upward. Such a positive EVA bias would be induced by the "double counting" of the firm's interest tax subsidy.

SLF's Levered Taxes and Tax Subsidies

Exhibit 6 shows how the taxes and tax subsidies might be calculated for SLF as a levered and unlevered firm, respectively. In simple terms, the exhibit shows that SLF's tax of $240 million is calculated by multiplying the 40% tax rate by the accounting net profit before-tax (NPBT) figure. However, the top portion of the exhibit also shows that the firm's $240 million tax can be packaged into two financial components — in particular, the $296 million in taxes due (UTAX) by SLF as an unlevered firm, *minus* the interest tax shield ($56 million) that the levered firm receives on the outstanding debt.

Moreover, the lower portion of Exhibit 6 reveals that the levered SLF receives tax subsidies that total some $136 million. This yearly benefit reflects the $80 million depreciation shield (0.4 × $200 million) and the previously mentioned interest tax subsidy. In contrast, as an unlevered firm, SLF receives only the $80 million depreciation tax subsidy. Other things the same, this is why the levered SLF could trade at a higher value than its unlevered business risk equivalent.

COST OF CAPITAL ESTIMATION CHALLENGES

The above discussion on the composition of the levered firm's cash flows reveals that EVA can be a challenging metric to estimate in practice. The popular view that EVA is "simply" the firm's after-tax operating profit less the dollar cost of capital employed in the business can now be seen as an understatement at best. These cash flow measurement issues can be expected to grow when moving from a simple income statement and balance sheet — like that of an SLF — to more complex, or real-time financial statements.

Aside from any further accounting difficulties that may arise when calculating EVA, there remains some meaningful "cost of capital" issues that can impact the estimation of this financial metric. In particular, Professor Merton Miller of the University of Chicago argues that even in a world of taxes with deductibility of debt interest expense, levered firms should still be priced as if they were equivalent business-risk unlevered firms.[7]

---

[7] See Merton H. Miller, "Debt and Taxes," *Journal of Finance* (May 1977).

Exhibit 6: SLF
Tax Reconciliation: Levered and Unlevered Firm

Tax on Levered Firm (LTAX):

$$
\begin{aligned}
\text{LTAX} \quad &= t\ \text{NPBT} \\
&= \text{UTAX} - \text{Interest Shield} \\
&= \text{UTAX} - t\ [\text{Interest Expense}] \\
&= 296 - 0.4\ [140] \\
&= 296 - 56 \\
&= \$240
\end{aligned}
$$

Tax on Unlevered Firm (UTAX):

$$
\begin{aligned}
\text{UTAX} \quad &= t\ [\text{EBITD} - Dp] \\
&= t\ [\text{EBITD}] - t\ Dp \\
&= 0.4\ [940] - 0.4\ [200] \\
&= 376 - 80 \\
&= \$296
\end{aligned}
$$

Levered Firm Tax Subsidy (LTSUB):

$$
\begin{aligned}
\text{LTSUB} \quad &= \text{UTSUB}^* + \text{Interest Shield} \\
&= t\ [\text{Depreciation}] + t\ [\text{Interest Expense}] \\
&= 0.4\ [200] + 0.4\ [140] \\
&= 80 + 56 \\
&= \$136
\end{aligned}
$$

*Unlevered Firm Tax Subsidy (UTSUB):

$$
\begin{aligned}
\text{UTSUB} \quad &= \text{Depreciation Shield}^{**} \\
&= 0.4\ [200] \\
&= \$80
\end{aligned}
$$

** The Interest Tax Subsidy difference of $56 (LTSUB less UTSUB) shows up in the $ Cost of Debt (step B) portion of the EVA Calculation.

In Miller's well-known "Debt and Taxes" model, the pre-tax rate of interest on taxable corporate bonds rises in the capital market to a level that offsets any perceived gains from corporate leverage at the firm level. As a result, he reestablishes the "capital structure irrelevance" predictions of the original MM (Miller-Modigliani) model. These powerful principles of corporation finance suggest that corporate debt policy has no meaningful impact on the value of the firm. Hence, in this modern view, the levered firm's cost of capital is the same as the capital cost estimate for the equivalent business-risk unlevered firm.

To illustrate the EVA-importance of Miller's arguments in a more direct way, consider a familiar (to students of corporate finance) expression of the relationship between the cost of capital for the levered and unlevered firms. In this context, the firm's after-tax capital cost can be expressed in terms of the post-tax cost of capital for the equivalent business-risk unlevered firm (UCOC), and the expected tax benefit available to the company from the interest tax subsidy. In more formal terms, the levered firm's cost of capital (LCOC) can be represented as:

$$LCOC = UCOC \ [1 - t(D/C)]$$

where, UCOC is the unlevered firm's cost of capital, t is the *effective* debt tax subsidy rate, and (D/C) is the firm's "target" debt-to-capital ratio.

In the "Debt and Taxes" model, Miller argues that competition in the market for taxable and tax-exempt bonds dictates that the levered firm's cost of capital (LCOC) will be the same as the capital cost for the unlevered firm, UCOC. This implies that the firm's weighted debt tax sudsidy term, t (D/C), in the cost of capital formulation must be zero. In effect, Miller's pioneering work throughout the years reveals that corporate debt policy *per se* has no impact whatsoever on the firm's after-tax cost of capital, and therefore, its overall market capitalization.

Suffice it to say that the effective debt tax subsidy rate, t, that applies in the real world is considerably lower than the stated corporate tax rate that managers and investors might incorrectly use in the estimation of EVA. EVA estimates that are calculated in this simple way would of course be biased upward. This measurement error would result from the inherent downward bias in the levered firm's cost of capital due to the presumed debt-tax subsidy. Moreover, unless this seemingly favorable interest tax subsidy benefit to the levered firm's cost of capital is noticed by investors, then the debt-induced EVA bias could lead to an overly-optimistic assessment of the market value of the firm and its outstanding shares.

Impact of CAPM Anomalies

A second, and perhaps more problematic, cost of capital issue arises in the context of estimating the required return on the firm's levered stock. In principle, the Stern-Stewart approach of using CAPM to estimate the firm's anticipated equity cost seems reasonable enough because this model is an integral component of the modern theory of finance. As mentioned before, William Sharpe shared in the Nobel Prize in Economic Sciences (along with Harry Markowitz and Merton Miller) in 1990 for his efforts in the early development of this investment model.

In recent years, however, CAPM has been challenged by many empirical studies that question the validity of the expected return-risk predictions of the model. In this asset pricing framework, *beta* is considered to be the systematic (or relative) risk factor that drives the required rate of return on the (levered) firm's outstanding common stock. Stocks of companies with high betas — due, perhaps, to volatile operating and/or leverage conditions — should offer relatively high expected returns, while stocks of firms with low betas should offer comparably lower anticipated returns.

However, the empirical evidence does not seem to verify the predictions of the model. In a major long-term study using common stock returns over the

1941-1990 period, Fama and French conclude that the celebrated CAPM relationship between average returns and beta risk is "weak," and "perhaps nonexistent." They also find that "two easily measured variables," including size (equity capitalization) and price-to-book value provide a "simple and powerful characterization of the cross-section of average stock returns for the 1963-1990 period."[8]

In addition, in the Winter 1995 issue of the *Journal of Portfolio Management*, the author reported an inverse relationship between beta risk and average portfolio returns during the 13-year period from 1980 to 1992.[9] During this period, the low volatility (beta and return standard deviation) stocks of companies with both large and small equity capitalization were the best performing U.S. equity investments. Moreover, it is well documented in the finance literature that the common stocks of small companies have on the average outperformed the stocks of large firms in a way that cannot be explained by the CAPM. This so-called "small firm effect," seemed particularly pervasive during the calendar month of January.

SUMMARY

This chapter shows how to estimate EVA in the context of basic financial statements. Because of the depreciation and interest tax subsidy issues, it is helpful to identify the after-tax operating cash flow that is available to the shareholders in the equivalent business-risk *unlevered* firm, and the interest tax subsidy that is uniquely available to the securityholders of the *levered* firm. Because of the tax subsidy issues, the illustration indicated that even with simple income statement and balance sheet data, the EVA calculation can be a challenging task.

In addition to accounting complexities that may arise when estimating EVA, there remains some daunting theoretical and empirical issues pertaining to the cost of capital. In particular, the cost of capital formula presumes that the firm has already found its "target" debt level or optimal capital structure. Yet, the modern capital structure principles (Miller's Debt and Tax" model, for example) upon which the MVA and EVA models rest indicate that both levered and unlevered firms should trade for the same overall market value. In this efficient market setting, the overall cost of capital for the levered firm (LCOC) is the same as the cost of equity capital for the equivalent business-risk unlevered firm.

In practice, the firm's debt tax subsidy rate, t, may range from zero up to the corporate tax rate. A naive application of the corporate tax rate in estimating the levered firm's interest tax subsidy would result in a downward bias in the firms dollar cost of capital. In turn, EVA estimates calculated in this way would

---

[8] See Eugene F. Fama and Kenneth R. French, "The Cross Section of Expected Stock Returns," *Journal of Finance* (June 1992).

[9] See James L. Grant, "A Yield Effect in Common Stock Returns," *Journal of Portfolio Management* (Winter 1995).

be biased upward. Unless the EVA estimation error is noticed by investors, it may impart an upward bias in the firm's market value added (MVA). If this happens, then its aggregate market value would be optimistically biased.

In addition, the primary reason for using EVA analysis when making corporate investment decisions is that it explicitly recognizes the importance of the cost of equity capital. Unfortunately, the CAPM approach to estimating the firm's equity cost is plagued by some significant empirical anomalies. On balance, these irregularities suggest that beta alone is not sufficiently robust to describe the expected return-risk relationship for investors operating in real-time capital markets.

On the positive side, the benefits of using EVA analysis seems to outweigh the hopefully minor cost arising from misestimation. This affirmative statement is based on the fact that EVA is, in principle, the *annualized* equivalent of the firm's aggregate net present value. As mentioned in Chapter 2, managerial decisions that enhance the ability of the firm to generate EVA for the future must in turn enhance shareholder wealth in the present. These EVA and MVA improvements are consistent with the shareholder wealth maximization imperative. Moreover, the empirical irregularities that challenge the CAPM are problematic for any corporate finance and investment model that attempts to measure the economic source of the firm's market value-added.

Chapter 4
Financial Characteristics of Wealth Creators

The NPV model presented in Chapter 2 reveals that wealth creating firms have positive economic value added. This "good news" for the shareholders occurs when the firm's managers invest in real assets having an expected after-tax rate of return on capital (ROC) that exceeds the weighted average cost of capital (COC). Moreover, that managers can make wealth-maximizing investment decisions for all the shareholders by following the (positive) NPV rule is one of the major "Separation Principles" of modern corporate finance.[1]

MVA AND EVA: TOP TEN U.S. WEALTH CREATORS

Some real-world insight on the wealth creation process can be seen by focusing on those firms that have in fact created wealth. Exhibit 1 presents the 1994 MVA and EVA characteristics of the "top-ten" U.S. wealth creators that were listed in the 1995 Performance 1000 Universe. The exhibit suggests that these wealth creators have large positive corporate valuations (MVA) because, in principle, *they should have*. With the exception of AT&T, Exhibit 1 reports that nine of the top ten U.S. wealth creators had contemporaneously positive MVA and EVA at year-end 1994. This positive association between the two measures of corporate financial success indicates that the currently favorable EVA news conveys positive news to investors about the firm's ability to generate economic value-added for the future.

Coca-Cola and General Electric top the 1994 wealth creator list with $60.8 billion and $52 billion in market value added, respectively. This means that the aggregate market value of the two firms exceeded the book capital employed in the businesses by these large NPV figures. As reported by Stern-Stewart, Coca-Cola and General Electric also occupied the top two MVA positions in the Performance 1000 Universe at year-end 1993 — this time, with General Electric boasting

---

[1] A rigorous treatment of "Separation Principles" of modern corporation finance can be found in Eugene F. Fama and Merton H. Miller, *The Theory of Finance* (New York: Holt, Rinehart, and Winston 1972).

Separation Principle I suggests that operating and financing decisions are separable. This principle has corporate-wide EVA implications because it implies that — in an efficient capital market — the cost of capital is independent of the method of financing.

Likewise, Separation Principle II indicates that corporate investment decisions can be made independently of shareholders' "tastes" for present and future consumption. Accordingly, in a well-functioning capital market, positive NPV (or, positive EVA) projects are wealth-increasing for *all* the firm's owners, while negative NPV projects destroy overall shareholder wealth.

an NPV value of $56 billion and Coca-Cola's MVA of $53.7 billion. Moreover, Exhibit 1 shows that Coke outdistanced AT&T and Motorola (firms 9 and 10) by some $38 billion in market value-added.

Exhibit 1 also points to some interesting anomalies in the MVA and EVA relationship for large wealth creators. In particular, at $2.22 billion, Philip Morris (firm 7) has the highest reported EVA among the top ten wealth creators. In contrast, its reported MVA is considerably lower than that observed for the top five companies shown in the wealth creator list. This could mean that investors were relatively pessimistic about the tobacco and food product company's ability to generate substantially positive EVA in the future. On the other hand, it could mean that Philip Morris was comparatively undervalued in the capital market at year-end 1994.

Similarly, the exhibit shows that AT&T had currently negative EVA, −$196 million, in the presence of the large positive MVA, $22.5 billion. Like Philip Morris, two possible explanations seem consistent with this finding. At year-end 1994, investors may have been optimistic about this telecommunication firm's ability to generate positive EVA for the future. Alternatively, the contemporaneously negative association between the two financial measures may indicate that AT&T's outstanding debt *and* equity securities were somewhat overvalued at year-end 1994.

ROC and COC: Top Ten Wealth Creators

The source of the positive "economic value added" for the top ten wealth creators is shown in Exhibit 2. As expected, the exhibit shows that powerful wealth creators have an after-tax ROC that exceeds the weighted average COC. This observation is supported by large wealth creators like Coca-Cola (KO), Microsoft (MSFT), and Johnson & Johnson (JNJ) having after-tax ROC ratios that are considerably higher than their COC estimates. Indeed, the 1994 "residual return on capital (ROC less COC)" figures for the three large wealth creators were 25.5%, 33%, and 7% respectively.

Exhibit 1: Top Ten Wealth Creators in Performance 1000 Universe at Year-End 1994

Company	MVA*	EVA	Return on Capital (%)	Cost of Capital (%)
	(in U.S.$ Millions)			
Coca-Cola Company	60846	1184	35.49	10.00
General Electric Co.	52071	863	14.77	12.86
Wal-Mart Stores	34996	917	13.72	9.64
Merck Co., Inc.	31467	1124	19.45	12.81
Microsoft Corp.	29904	989	47.55	14.37
Procter & Gamble Co,	27830	615	13.92	11.14
Philip Morris Co., Inc.	27338	2222	16.30	10.83
Johnson & Johnson	24699	798	19.60	12.56
AT&T	22542	−196	10.08	10.37
Motorola, Inc.	21068	438	16.80	13.16

* MVA = Market Value of the Firm less the book capital employed in the business. In principle, MVA is also equal to the Present Value of the Firm's expected future EVA.

Exhibit 2: Return on Capital versus Cost of Capital: Top Ten Wealth Creators in Performance Universe at Year-End 1994

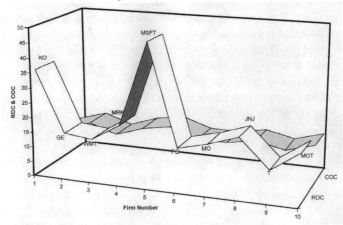

Exhibit 2 also shows that the 1994 ROC ratios for Coca-Cola, Microsoft, and Johnson & Johnson are considerably higher than the ROC ratio for General Electric and AT&T (aside from the firm's currently negative EVA). This favorable financial result happens because the former wealth creators are generating high returns on a relatively small amount of invested capital. For instance, Stern-Stewart report that Microsoft's 1994 ROC was 47.6% on a beginning of year operating capital of only $2.98 billion!

Coca-Cola and Johnson & Johnson had 1994 capital returns of 35.5% and 19.6% on invested capital of $7.39 billion and $11.35 billion, respectively. On the other hand, General Electric reported a 14.8% post-tax return on some $45 billion of "book capital" employed in the business. Moreover, AT&T's (sub-par) 10% ROC for 1994 was earned on a large operating capital base of $65.5 billion.

A closer look at Exhibit 2 suggests that the fluctuations in EVA estimates among the top ten wealth creators in the 1995 Performance Universe is determined primarily by the volatility in their after-tax ROC ratios. In this context, the individual COC figures are noticeably stable around the cross-sectional average rate of 11.8%. In contrast, the after-tax capital return (ROC) figures for the top ten wealth creators fluctuate sharply about the cross-sectional average of 20.8%. Moreover, the standard deviation on the ten reported ROC ratios is 11.6%, while this volatility measure is only 1.6% for the ten listed (Exhibit 2) COC ratios.

MVA AND EVA: 50 LARGE WEALTH CREATORS

Exhibit 3 expands the wealth creator focus by showing the relationship between the MVA-to-capital and EVA-to-capital ratios for the 50 largest "wealth creators" in the Performance 1000 Universe at year-end 1994. As expected, the exhibit indicates that a strong (linear) relationship exists between the twin measures of "economic value added" for the top performing firms. When the EVA-to-capital ratio is both large and positive, the corresponding MVA-to-capital ratio is high and positive in value. Likewise, when the EVA-to-capital ratio is low and negative for these large firms, the corresponding MVA-to-capital ratio is low in value.

A closer look at Exhibit 3 reveals that 34 of the 50 (or, 68%) largest wealth creators at year-end 1994 had jointly positive EVA- and MVA-to-capital ratios. This finding indicates that the firm's most recently announced EVA makes a positive contribution to the firm's overall corporate valuation, as measured empirically by the MVA-to-capital ratio. This positive EVA momentum is clearly "good news" as it conveys windfall capital gains to the firm's shareholders.

In addition, the 16 out of 50 large "wealth creators" in the exhibit with positive MVA-to-capital ratios in the presence of currently negative EVA-to-capital ratios show that future growth opportunities play a *doubly* meaningful role in the valuation of these U.S. large capitalization firms. That is, if the capital market were efficient at year-end 1994, then investors were also optimistic about the future ability of the 16 firms having currently adverse EVA figures to generate economic value-added for the future. In the absence of this investor optimism, the securities of these firms would have been overvalued in the capital market at that time.

The empirical observations shown in Exhibit 3 are reinforced in the statistical results that follow. In particular, Exhibit 4 estimates the linear association between the MVA-to-capital ratio (dependent variable) and the EVA-to-capital ratio (explanatory variable) for the 50 largest U.S. wealth creators at year-end 1994. With an EVA "beta" (or slope coefficient) of 23.67, and a t-statistic of 11.84, the exhibit shows that the EVA-to-capital ratio for powerful wealth creators is a highly significant financial variable.

Exhibit 3: MVA-to-Capital versus EVA-to-Capital Ratio: 50 Largest Wealth Creators in Performance Universe at Year-End 1994

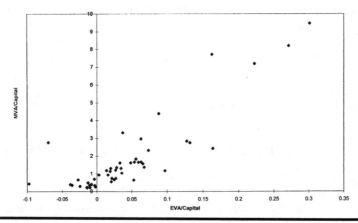

Exhibit 4: Regression Statistics for 50 Largest Wealth Creators in Performance 1000 Universe at Year-End 1994

MVA/Capital = 0.78 + 23.67 EVA/Capital
(t-value)   (4.48) (11.84)

Adjusted R^2 = 73.97%
N = 50 Firms

Exhibit 5: ROC versus COC: 50 Largest Wealth Creators in Performance Universe at Year-End 1994

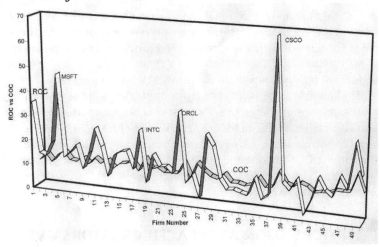

The cross-sectional regression statistics for 1994 also reveal that 74% of the movement in the MVA-to-capital ratios for top-performing large firms is explained by variations in the EVA-to-capital factor. Moreover, this high adjusted R^2-value in the MVA and EVA relationship for the 50 largest wealth creators is consistent with the 83% of variation explained figure reported in the recent Grant study for year-end 1993.[2]

ROC and COC: 50 Large Wealth Creators

Exhibit 5 reveals the economic source of the positive relationship between the MVA and EVA measures shown in the previous exhibit. Specifically, Exhibit 5 presents a comparison of the after-tax ROC and COC for the 50 largest "wealth creators" in the Performance Universe at year-end 1994. As predicted by the classic NPV model, the exhibit reveals that wealth creating firms have positive market value

---

[2] See James L. Grant, "Foundations of EVA for Investment Managers," *Journal of Portfolio Management* (Fall 1996).

added because their after-tax rate of return on invested capital exceeds the weighted average cost of capital. In other words, these powerful wealth creators have a positive residual (or surplus) return on capital where ROC is largely higher than COC.

Taken together, the large positive residual return on capital ratios implied in the ROC and COC findings in Exhibit 5 lead to the large positive EVA-to-capital ratios shown in Exhibit 4. In turn, the positive EVA-to-capital information is clearly "good news" to the firm's shareholders as it generates sizable improvements in the firm's overall corporate valuation. In this context, the cross-sectional findings for the large wealth creators are consistent with the theoretical predictions of the NPV model — whereby, the firm's EVA (and, therefore MVA) is positive when the anticipated residual return on capital (ROC minus COC) is greater than zero.

From a statistical perspective, the empirical connection between the MVA-to-capital ratio and the residual return on capital measure for the 50 largest U.S. wealth creators in the Performance Universe is strongly reinforced in the multiple regression statistics reported in Exhibit 6. With a slope coefficient of 0.161, and a t-statistic of 10.94, the surplus return on capital factor (ROC-COC) has a significant positive impact on the firm's MVA-to-capital ratio.

The multiple regression results for 1994 also indicate that variability in the cost of capital among large U.S. "wealth creators" is a statistically significant, yet relatively smaller, factor in assessing why these firms generated market value added for the shareholders. This latter observation may result in part because the variability in the COC among the 50 largest wealth creators at year-end 1994 is noticeably small, as seen in Exhibit 5, in comparison with the cross-sectional volatility in the after-tax ROC ratios.

A STATISTICAL LOOK AT WEALTH CREATORS OVER TIME

In view of the highly significant findings observed for powerful wealth creators during 1994, it is helpful to see if the MVA- and EVA-to-capital relationship is empirically robust for other years. In this context, Exhibit 7 presents a time series display of the regression statistics that were estimated between the two financial measures for the large U.S. wealth creators during the 1990 to 1994 period. The sample portfolios consist of the 50 largest wealth creators that were listed in the 1995 Performance Universe after adjustment for a few yearly MVA and EVA (data) omissions.

Exhibit 6: Multiple Regression Statistics for 50 Largest Wealth Creators in Performance 1000 Universe at Year-End 1994

MVA/Capital = −1.16 + 0.179 COC + 0.161 [ROC − COC]
(t-value)   (-1.42)   (2.47)   (10.94)

Adjusted R^2 = 79.5
N = 50 Firms

Exhibit 7: MVA- and EVA-to-Capital Regression Statistics: 50 Largest Wealth Creators in Performance 1000 Universe

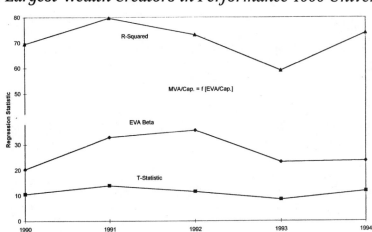

Exhibit 7 provides *yearly* estimates of the percentage of MVA-to-capital variation explained (adjusted R^2), the EVA-beta (slope), and the *t*-statistic, respectively, that emerged from the linear regressions over the 5-year reporting period. The exhibit reveals that the percentage of MVA variation explained by the EVA-to-capital factor for large U.S. wealth creators varies over time from about 60% to 80%. The average R^2 value for the 50 firms, 71%, shows that the size-adjusted EVA measure of corporate financial success is a significant factor for wealth creators.

Exhibit 7 also shows that the "EVA-beta" ranges from a yearly low of about 20 in 1990 to a high sensitivity of 36 in 1992. The 5-year average for these reported slope measures was 27.16. Moreover, this time series view that the MVA- and EVA-to-capital relationship for large U.S. wealth creators is empirically robust is also supported by the average *t*-statistic, 11.29, on the estimated yearly EVA betas.

Additionally, Exhibit 8 shows the yearly regression results for the 50 largest wealth creators that emerged from a regression analysis based on the *unadjusted* MVA and EVA variables. These tests reveal that although the estimated EVA-betas (slope measures) are statistically significant for wealth creators in the "raw regressions," the percentage of MVA yearly variation explained by the dollar-based EVA factor is considerably lower than the R^2 figures observed in Exhibit 7.

In this context, the *t*-statistics on the EVA-betas in the unadjusted regressions ranged from a (significant) low of 2.26 in 1993 to a high of 7.46 in 1990. The 5-year average of the *t*-values from the dollar-based regressions was 4.48 (with an average EVA-beta of 7.11). In turn, the yearly percentage of MVA variation explained by the *unadjusted* EVA factor ranged from only 7.7% in 1993 to a high of 52.71% in 1990. On average, it seems that the dollar-based EVA variable explains about 27% of the cross-sectional variability in the unadjusted MVA for large wealth creators.

Exhibit 8: MVA and EVA Regression Statistics: 50 Largest Wealth Creators in Performance 1000 Universe

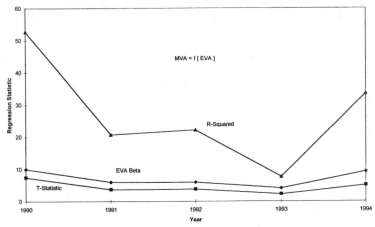

Exhibit 9: Regression Statistics for First Decile of Performance 1000 Universe at Year End 1994

MVA/Capital = 0.96 + 18.57 EVA/Capital
(t-statistic)   (7.25) (14.26)

Adjusted R^2 = 67.37%
N = 99 Firms

The regression findings using the unadjusted EVA factor as the independent variable are statistically meaningful. However, in practical terms, they are consistently lower than the yearly MVA statistics observed in Exhibit 7 with the EVA-to-capital ratio employed as the explanatory factor. Taken together, these findings reveal that real corporate profits should be measured relative to the *amount* of capital that is required to generate that level of profitability.

MVA AND EVA: TOP DECILE WEALTH CREATORS

Finally, Exhibit 9 reports the linear regression results for the first decile of the Performance 1000 Universe for 1994. This partial look at the *decile* characteristics of companies listed in the 1995 Performance universe will be expanded upon in the next chapter, where the MVA and EVA focus is primarily on the financial characteristics of wealth destroyers.

With a slope measure of 18.57, and a *t*-statistic of 14.26, the EVA-to-capital factor has a highly significant impact on the MVA-to-capital ratios for the first decile companies (99 firms, with companion data) listed in the Performance Universe at year-end 1994. Also, with an R^2-value at 67%, it is interesting to see that the strength of the linear association between the MVA-to-capital and EVA-to-capital ratios for the first decile companies is still quite high, especially when compared to the 74% of MVA variation explained for the top 50 firms reported in Exhibit 4.

The empirical findings for wealth creators presented in this chapter are also interesting in view of the fact that the R^2-figure in the MVA-to-capital and EVA-to-capital regression for the entire Performance Universe (990 firms, with companion data) at year-end 1994 is, precisely, *zero*. Indeed, it seems that for 1994 the aggregation of all firms — including wealth creators, firms that are striving to create wealth, and wealth wasters — has masked the powerful *cross-sectional* pricing happenings in the overall marketplace.

SUMMARY

This chapter looks at the empirical evidence for large U.S. wealth creators in the Performance 1000 Universe. Although the research focus is primarily on major companies that have improved shareholder wealth, the real purpose of the chapter is to assess the *maximum* pricing strength of the EVA metric. If the EVA factor were found to be insignificant in this grouping of firms, then there would be no reason whatsoever to hold this metric out to the financial community as a relevant measure of corporate success. On the other hand, if EVA is in fact a robust factor in explaining the volatility in the firm's market value added, then managers and investors alike should pay close attention to the information content of this corporate performance measure.

The empirical evidence for large wealth creators is consistent with the predictions of the classic NPV model. The annual regression statistics estimated during the 1990 to 1994 period show that the EVA-to-capital ratio explains some 60% to 80% of the volatility in MVA-to-capital ratios for the 50 largest U.S. wealth creators in the Performance 1000 Universe. On the other hand, the dollar-based MVA and EVA regressions for these firms over the 5-year reporting interval gave a somewhat weaker financial message .

In particular, the empirical evidence for powerful wealth creators indicates that the dollar-based MVA and EVA relationship is statistically significant. However, in practical terms, the percentage of MVA-variation explained on the sample portfolios of 50 wealth creators during the years 1990 to 1994 is considerably lower than the adjusted R^2-values observed in the size-adjusted MVA-to-Capital and EVA-to-Capital regressions. Armed with this empirical knowledge, it is now time to look at the MVA and EVA characteristics of those firms that have unfortunately destroyed shareholder wealth.

Chapter 5

Financial Characteristics of Wealth Destroyers

The NPV model of corporate finance also has some powerful implications for wealth wasters. In this context, the model predicts that firms having negative expected EVA will ultimately destroy shareholder wealth. As shown in Chapter 2, the shareholders' wealth loss is caused by the firm's negative anticipated "residual return on capital (RROC)." In this adverse situation, the firm's average after-tax return on capital (ROC) is less than the weighted average cost of capital (COC). Indeed, the model shows that *seemingly* profitable companies in the traditional accounting sense can destroy wealth if their positive post-tax capital return falls short of expected after-tax capital costs.[1]

Knowledge of the financial characteristics of wealth destroyers can be particularly helpful to both corporate managers and investors. Armed with a clear understanding of the MVA and EVA linkage for firms that have in fact destroyed wealth, corporate managers can use this information to avoid the kind of managerial mistakes that give rise to troubled firms. Likewise, by focusing on the modern EVA metric, the managers of troubled firms can see why their relatively low capital return investments (positive ROC that falls below COC) have led to the currently adverse MVA situation.

In the absence of a concerted effort by the managers of troubled firms to generate a positive residual return on capital (RROC), the firm's debt and equity capitalization will remain far below the firm's wealth-maximization potential. Indeed, without a clear focus on how to measure real economic profits (EVA), the troubled firm's corporate managers may inadvertently invite a hostile "tender offer" bid from a more wealth conscious (MVA) management team.

Information about a firm's EVA momentum is important for investors too. By focusing research efforts on this financial metric, securities analysts may gain some meaningful pricing insight on the likely direction of *both* the firm's outstanding debt and equity securities. In the case of troubled firms, investors may be able to see the forthcoming capital losses that will result from managerial decisions having negative EVA consequences.

The NPV model predicts that firms having negative EVA momentum will see their bond and stock prices decline over time. Stock prices decline because

---

[1] It is important to emphasize that EVA is positive when the after-tax capital return is higher than the weighted average cost of debt *and* equity. Firms having positive post-tax capital returns that lie below the cost of capital will still destroy wealth, even though their capital returns are sufficient to cover the anticipated cost of debt. This corporate finance consideration is at the heart of what the "EVA Revolution" is all about.

the negative EVA outlook leads to a reduction in the *intrinsic value* of the firm's future stream of real earnings. Likewise, bond prices fall because the negative EVA happenings lead to "credit downgrades" in the firm's outstanding debt securities. The investment importance of looking at firms having both negative and positive EVA characteristics is covered extensively in future chapters. For now, it's time to gain some empirical understanding of the MVA and EVA linkages for firms that have — in retrospect — destroyed shareholder wealth.

MVA AND EVA: TOP TEN U.S. WEALTH DESTROYERS

Exhibit 1 presents the MVA and EVA findings for the ten largest wealth destroyers listed in the 1995 Performance 1000 Universe. Among the year-end 1994 findings, the exhibit shows that wealth destroyers have low corporate valuations because *they should have*. In particular, with the noticeable exceptions of Chrysler and Ford, eight of the top ten wealth destroyers had currently negative EVA in the presence of adverse MVA figures. The negative market value added figures range from -$2.32 billion for Occidental Petroleum Corporation down to -$17.8 billion of cumulative wealth destruction for General Motors.

    Although the after-tax ROC figures are mostly positive in Exhibit 1, these firms are considered wealth destroyers because their capital returns fall short of the weighted average COC. For instance, the negative MVA values for IBM and General Motors (−$8.86 billion and −$17.8 billion, respectively) result in part because their after-tax return on capital ranges from only 55% to 79% of the reported cost of capital figures. At −6.99%, it is also interesting to see that more than five years after the largest hostile takeover in U.S. history, RJR Nabisco Holdings is still showing a negative "residual return on capital."

Exhibit 1: Top Ten Wealth Destroyers in Performance 1000 Universe at Year-End 1994 (in US$ Millions)

Company	MVA*	EVA	Return on Capital (%)	Cost of Capital (%)
Occidental Petroleum Group	−2,320	−1,306	2.71	10.23
Federated Department Stores	−2,598	−120	6.99	8.82
K Mart Corp.	−2,630	−1,485	3.51	11.50
Westinghouse Electric	−2,783	−659	4.07	10.57
Chrysler Corp.	−3,177	2,993	30.67	13.17
Digital Equipment	−4,684	−2,992	−9.56	12.87
IBM	−8,864	−3,019	5.41	9.77
RJR Nabisco Holdings	−11,761	−2,268	5.95	12.94
Ford Motor Company	−13,757	985	14.86	12.87
General Motors Corp.	−17,803	−2,044	8.59	10.92

* MVA = Market Value of the Firm less the Book Capital employed in the business. In principle, MVA is also equal to the Present Value of the Firm's Expected Future EVA.

Chrysler Corporation and Ford Motor Corporation stand out as noticeable empirical exceptions to the more general observation that negative MVA is typically associated with negative EVA. For instance, Exhibit 1 shows that Chrysler had currently positive EVA, $2.99 billion, in the presence of its large negative MVA, −$3.18 billion. This apparent anomaly in the MVA and EVA relationship for the two automakers has (at least) two possible financial explanations.

In view of the large negative MVA values (−$13.76 billion and −$3.18 billion, respectively) for Ford Motor Company and Chrysler, it seems that investors — operating in an efficient capital market — were exceedingly pessimistic about the ability of the two automakers to generate positive economic value added (EVA) for the future. On the other hand, if the capital market were largely inefficient, then the adverse MVA values for 1994 would indicate that the outstanding debt and equity securities of these firms were significantly undervalued (due to the positive EVA) in the marketplace at that time.

ROC and COC: Top Ten Wealth Destroyers

Exhibit 2 shows a comparison of the after-tax ROC versus the COC for the top ten wealth destroyers in the Performance 1000 Universe at year end 1994. The findings reported in this exhibit are important for at least two reasons. First, the U.S. wealth destroyers shown here have negative net present values (NPV) even though their ROC ratios are *mostly* positive. In this context, the ten largest wealth wasters in the Performance Universe for 1994 had an average capital return of only 7.3%. Meanwhile, the average cost of capital for the ten firms was 11.4% at that time.

Exhibit 2: Return on Capital versus Cost of Capital: Ten Largest Wealth Destroyers in Performance 1000 Universe for 1994

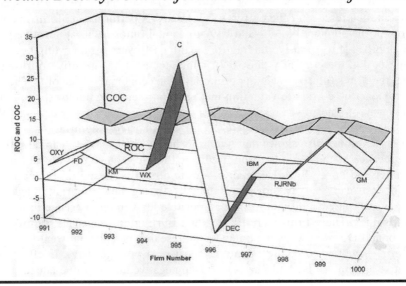

For recent wealth wasters — like General Motors, IBM, and RJR Nabisco Holdings — the financial chain of events seems to go like this: at −4.10%, the negative average residual return on capital (11.4%-7.3%) leads to the negative average EVA for the firms listed in Exhibit 1. In turn, the current EVA announcement conveys negative information to investors about the firm's future ability to generate economic value added. If correct, then the adverse EVA anticipation results in a dramatic decline in the market value of the firm and its outstanding securities. This explanation is, in principle, the economic reasoning behind the large negative MVA figures for the wealth destroyers shown in Exhibit 1.

Second, the reported findings suggest that the cross-sectional differences in the EVA estimates for the ten largest wealth destroyers at year-end 1994 were largely due to the cross variability in the after-tax return on capital. With a standard deviation of 10.2%, the ROC estimates are noticeably volatile about the 7.3% average figure for the ten firms reported in this exhibit. In contrast, the COC estimates appear quite stable about the average value of 11.4%. Indeed, at 10.2%, the cross-sectional standard deviation on the after-tax capital returns for the ten recent wealth wasters is considerably higher (6.8 times) than the 1.5% volatility in their cost of capital estimates.

EVA AND CORPORATE VALUATION:
50 LARGE WEALTH DESTROYERS

In light of the empirical findings for the ten largest wealth wasters, it is helpful for managers and investors alike to see if the negative MVA and EVA association is present in a larger sample of firms. In this context, Exhibit 3 graphs the MVA-to-capital and EVA-to-capital ratios for the 50 largest U.S. wealth destroyers in the Performance 1000 Universe at year-end 1994.

As expected, the exhibit reports consistently negative MVA-to-capital ratios in the presence of the currently adverse EVA performance. In this context, 45 out of the 50 paired MVA- and EVA-to-capital ratios occur at negative points in Exhibit 3. This pervasive finding for wealth destroyers is interesting because it suggests that the currently poor EVA announcement has negative information about the firm's future growth opportunities. The economic source of this adverse EVA impact on corporate valuation must in some sense be due to shareholder's assessment of a negative "residual return on capital," whereby, the after-tax ROC falls short of the weighted average COC for wealth destroying firms.

Exhibit 3 also shows that five firms had positive EVA-to-capital ratios in the presence of the negative capital-adjusted MVA values. Two of the firms — Chrysler and Ford Motor Company — were already covered in the ten largest wealth destroyers' survey shown in Exhibit 1. Among the forty firms added to the sample, only three additional firms had positive EVA in the presence of negative MVA values. These firms were FINA, Inc.; Burlington Industries, Equity; and, McDonnell Douglas. Thus, on balance, the research reveals that wealth destroying firms have low corporate valuations because *they should have.* In effect, their negative anticipated EVA ultimately leads to negative market value-added.

Exhibit 3: MVA-to-Capital versus EVA-to-Capital Ratio: 50 Largest Wealth Destroyers in Performance Universe for 1994

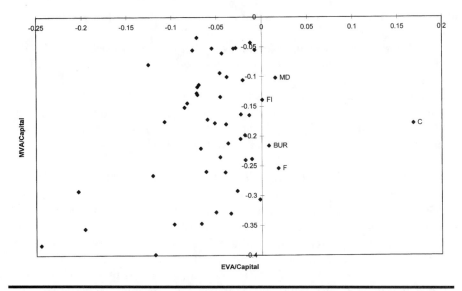

The empirical findings for the 50 wealth destroyers are also interesting when compared to the findings for wealth creators. In Chapter 4, it was demonstrated that while the MVA and EVA relationship is empirically robust for wealth creators, some 32% (16 out of 50) of the sample had negative EVA-to-capital ratios in the presence of the contemporaneously positive MVA. This seemingly anomalous finding for the wealth creators was explained (in an efficient market context) by recognizing that investors were optimistic about the ability of these firms to generate positive economic value added for the future — even though their current EVA-to-capital ratios were negative.

In view of this finding, Exhibit 3 points to a potential pricing asymmetry in the way that investors value the currently announced EVA for wealth creators and wealth destroyers. In this context, the exhibit shows that only 10% (5 out of 50) of the firms in the so-called wealth destroyer sample had positive EVA-to-capital ratios in the presence of negative MVA-to-capital ratios. In contrast, some 32% (16 out of 50) of the top 50 wealth creators had negative EVA-to-capital ratios in view of positive MVA-to-capital figures. In other words, 90% of the 50 largest wealth destroyers at year end 1994 had contemporaneously negative EVA- and MVA-to-capital ratios, while 68% of the wealth creator sample had both positive MVA- and EVA-to-capital ratios.

Taken together, these findings seem consistent with a pricing asymmetry where (1) the firm's *currently* announced EVA has a greater pricing weight for wealth wasters than it does for wealth creators and (2) the capital market is far more willing to take a chance on the *future* EVA prospects for growth-oriented firms in comparison with that of currently troubled firms. Indeed, in the case of negative MVA firms like Chrysler, Ford, and McDonnell Douglas (Exhibit 3), managerial initiatives toward generating positive EVA seem to have fallen on investors' deaf ears.

From a general perspective, it may be that financially troubled firms suffer from an abundance of "managerial noise." In effect, the clattering of conflicting financial sounds can prevent investors from either hearing or, worse yet, believing the firm's present attempts to generate economic value-added. Corporate managers in firms having serious financial difficulties must therefore make a concerted effort to convince the shareholders that the managerial actions they are taking will enhance the troubled firm's overall market value-added.

Statistical Results for 50 Large Wealth Destroyers

The strength of the statistical association between the MVA and EVA metrics for the 50 largest wealth destroyers in the 1995 Performance 1000 Universe is reported in Exhibit 4. As with the reported regression statistics for wealth creators in Chapter 4, the exhibit reports the relevant EVA-beta (slope measure), t-statistic, and the adjusted R^2-value in the linear estimation.

With a slope measure of 0.52 (EVA beta), and t-statistic of 2.34, Exhibit 4 shows that the EVA-to-capital factor (explanatory variable) has a statistically significant impact on the MVA-to-capital ratio (dependent variable) for the 50 U.S. wealth destroyers. However, in light of the wide scatter of the negative MVA- and EVA-to-capital points shown in Exhibit 3, it is not surprising to see that the percentage of MVA variation explained by the EVA-to-capital variable is noticeably weak.

At 8.35%, the adjusted R^2-value reported in Exhibit 4 is considerably lower than the 74% figure observed in Chapter 4 for the 50 largest U.S. wealth creators. Moreover, the EVA-beta (at 0.52) that emerges in the cross-section for large wealth destroyers is dramatically lower than the 23.67 sensitivity measure observed for the 50 comparable wealth creators. This reduced responsiveness of the size-adjusted MVA ratio to EVA changes for wealth destroyers may be due to the "noisy markets" argument for troubled firms.

Exhibit 4: Regression Statistics for 50 Largest Wealth Destroyers in Performance 1000 Universe at Year-End 1994

MVA/Capital = –0.16 + 0.52 EVA/Capital
(t-value)   (-8.94)   (2.34)

Adjusted R^2 = 8.35%
N = 50 Firms

Exhibit 5: Return on Capital versus Cost of Capital: 50 Largest Wealth Destroyers in Performance Universe for 1994

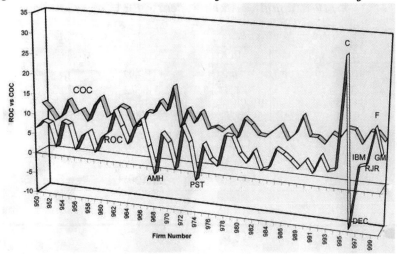

ROC and COC: 50 Large Wealth Destroyers

Exhibit 5 provides some further insight into the pricing characteristics of wealth wasters. The graph shows the after-tax ROC and COC for the 50 largest U.S. wealth destroyers at year-end 1994. Among the findings, the visual display reveals that recent wealth wasters with negative capital returns — such as Amdahl, Digital Equipment, and Petrie Stores — and major corporate players with currently positive, yet low capital returns — like General Motors, IBM, and RJR Nabisco — have consistently negative residual returns (RROC).

In this context, Exhibit 5 shows that 90% (45 out of 50) of the largest wealth destroyers at year-end 1994 had post-tax capital returns (ROC) that fell short of the capital costs (COC). From an efficient market perspective, these abnormal return announcements must have conveyed negative information to investors about the firms future growth opportunities. As a result, this negative signal led to a lowering of the market value of the firm and its outstanding debt and equity securities.

Chrysler Corporation and to a lesser degree, Ford Motor Company, stand out among the crowd of 50 firms as noticeable exceptions to the more general rule that wealth destroyers have a negative expected residual return on capital. Moreover, that wealth destroyers had mostly low capital returns when measured relative to the weighted average cost of capital during 1994 is consistent with the empirical findings reported in the author's recent study for 1993.[2]

---

[2] See James L. Grant, "Foundations of EVA for Investment Managers," *Journal of Portfolio Management* (Fall 1996).

Exhibit 6: Regression Statistics for Selected Deciles in Performance 1000 Universe at Year-End 1994
MVA/Capital = Alpha + Beta × EVA/Capital

Decile Number	Intercept	EVA Beta*	Adjusted R^2
1	0.96	18.57	67.37%
	(7.25)	(14.26)	
5	1.14	11.72	39.74%
	(9.16)	(8.06)	
6	0.90	2.99	10.57%
	(12.95)	(3.55)	
10	−0.12	0.46	7.47%
	(−9.46)	(3.00)	

* t-values reported in parenthesis.

MVA AND EVA: DECILE CHARACTERISTICS OF THE PERFORMANCE UNIVERSE

It is also helpful for corporate managers and investors to have knowledge of the MVA and EVA relationship across the general spectrum of companies listed in the Performance 1000 Universe. This empirical perspective can be obtained by looking at the pricing characteristics of sample portfolios of firms that have created wealth, firms that are striving to enhance wealth, and firms that have destroyed wealth. In this context, Exhibit 6 reports the linear regression statistics for selected MVA deciles of the Performance 1000 Universe at year-end 1994. The reported results are based on sample portfolios of firms having jointly listed MVA and EVA data in the first decile, fifth decile, sixth decile, and tenth decile.[3]

The regression performance summaries are interesting in a number of financial respects. In particular, Exhibit 6 shows that the EVA-to-capital ratio has a statistically significant impact on the MVA-to-capital ratio for the average firm in *each* of the reported deciles. In this context, the t-statistic on the EVA beta for the four reported performance deciles is considerably higher than the benchmark

---

[3] The reported regression results for the fifth decile are *net* of the two companies with the largest positive *and* negative EVA-to-capital ratios. Without this data adjustment, the adjusted R^2 is 42.42% for fifth decile firms, while the regression slope estimate is −37.21. The *one* large negative outlier in the fifth decile seems to overshadow the evidently positive MVA and EVA relationship that is shown in the exhibit.

This same adjustment procedure for potential outlier bias in the sixth decile companies did not impact the statistical results in any meaningful way — as there were no unusual EVA-to-capital occurrences.

of "2" that is often used in practice to gauge the statistical significance of an explanatory variable.[4]

However, the exhibit also shows that the strength of the statistical association between the MVA-to-capital and EVA-to-capital ratio weakens as one moves down the MVA-ranked list of companies in the Performance 1000 Universe. In this context, the EVA factor explains some 67% of the cross-sectional variation in the 1994 MVA-to-capital ratios for the 100 largest companies in the survey. The percentage of MVA variation explained by the EVA factor then declines to about 40% and 11% for the average firms in the fifth and sixth deciles, respectively.

In light of the previously reported results for wealth wasters, it is not surprising to see that Exhibit 6 reveals that the percentage of MVA-variation explained for companies listed in the tenth (bottom) decile is only 7%. This low adjusted R^2-value for the average firm in the last decile of the Performance Universe is consistent with the 8.35% figure observed in Exhibit 4 for the 50 largest wealth destroyers at year-end 1994.

ROC and COC: A Closer Look at the "Middle of the Road" Firms

Finally, Exhibit 7 provides an interesting display of the after-tax ROC and COC for the U.S. firms listed in the sixth decile of the Performance Universe. This "middle of the road" portfolio of firms having a mix of both positive and negative residual capital returns (RROC) is interesting, especially when compared to the empirical relationship between these financial metrics for large wealth creators and destroyers.

On balance, the cross-decile financial characteristics of firms listed in the Performance 1000 Universe are consistent with the predictions of the classic NPV model. Wealth creators have mostly positive residual capital returns, while firms that ultimately destroy shareholder value have predominantly after-tax capital

---

[4] The recognition that EVA has a statistically significant impact on MVA in the *cross-section* of large U.S. capitalization firms should not be interpreted to mean that this metric is a better predictor of corporate performance than other traditional measures, such as revenue and earnings growth, or return on equity (ROE). Indeed, nothing has been said here about the "relative information content" of the EVA performance measure.

Moreover, in a recent study at the University of Washington, Gary C. Biddle, Robert M. Bowen, and James S. Wallace ("Evidence on the Relative and Incremental Information Content of EVA®, Residual Income, Earnings, and Operating Cash Flow," Working paper (University of Washington, 1996)) concluded that EVA does not have overall incremental information content when compared to other well-know measures of corporate profitability.

It is important to recognize that EVA is a "top down" approach to corporate valuation that is firmly rooted in financial theory. EVA utilizes key financial principles — such as net present value analysis and internal rate of return (IRR) comparisons with the weighted average cost of capital — in a way that is formally linked to shareholder wealth. It is also important to emphasize that if a firm cannot produce and sell a meaningful product or service — and thereby grow its revenue over time — then no amount of EVA (or other performance metric) prodding will be able to offset the firm's wealth-destroying fate.

returns (ROC) that — although generally positive — fall below the weighted average cost of capital. "Middle of the road firms" like those companies in the reported sixth decile of the Performance Universe have residual capital returns (RROC) that seem to fluctuate about the wealth-neutrality position of *zero*.

SUMMARY

This chapter focused on the empirical characteristic of firms that have destroyed wealth. Knowledge of the MVA and EVA characteristics of wealth wasters is important to corporate managers because it provides some meaningful insight into what *not to do* when making real investment decisions for the future. On this score, the empirical evidence for troubled firms provides financial managers with a clear message about the NPV implications of investing in negative EVA-generating activities — wealth is wasted when managers invest in projects having post-tax capital returns that fall short of the weighted average cost of debt and equity capital.

Knowledge of the financial characteristics of wealth destroyers (and creators) is also important to investment managers. In principle, wealth wasting firms having negative EVA announcements will notice that their bond *and* equity prices are falling in the marketplace as the "bad news" conveys windfall capital losses to the firm's security holders. Stock prices fall in anticipation of the reduced residual earnings outlook, while bond prices may decline in anticipation of "credit downgrades" in the firm's outstanding debt securities. As emphasized in Chapter 4, the opposite sequence of pricing events happens for firms that are creating wealth for their shareholders.

Exhibit 7: Return on Capital versus Cost of Capital: Sixth Decile of Performance Universe for 1994

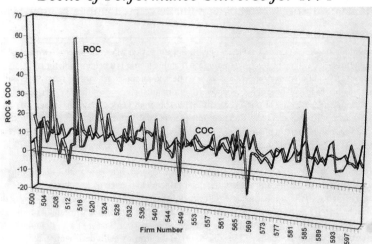

The empirical results for recent wealth destroyers are interesting when compared to the findings of wealth creators. In this context, some 90% of the bottom 50 MVA-ranked firms in the Performance Universe for 1994 had negative EVA-to-capital ratios. In the wealth creator sample (Chapter 4), some 68% of the 50 firms had *contemporaneously* positive MVA- and EVA-to-capital ratios. Among other things, this implies that the currently announced negative residual capital return for wealth destroyers is far more meaningful to investors than the announcement of presently negative EVA for wealth creators.

Moreover, with adjusted R^2 values that lie below 10% in the MVA and EVA regressions for wealth wasters, it seems that troubled firms are plagued by an abundance of "managerial noise." Indeed, the positive steps that corporate managers (for example, Chrysler and Ford in Exhibit 3) may be taking to turn the negative EVA situation around may sometimes not be enough to convince their concerned investors.

Chapter 6

Corporate Valuation Using EVA

In *The Theory of Finance*, Eugene F. Fama and Merton H. Miller explain how there are many equivalent ways of estimating the market value of a firm and its outstanding shares. Financial models that are designed to estimate a firm's stock price frequently include variations on the classic dividend discount model as well as the price relative approaches to equity valuation, such as price-to-earnings and price-to-book value. Investment models that focus on the aggregate value of a firm are generally based on some variation of the "free cash flow" approach to corporate valuation. However, since each of these pricing procedures is derived from the same (risk-adjusted) *equal rate of return principle*, they must, in principle, provide the same overall valuation results.[1]

One of the major benefits of using the EVA concept to value companies is that it gives both managers and investors a keen insight into how the firm derives its overall net present value. In contrast, the familiar DDMs (dividend discount models) and price relative (price-to-earnings and price-to-book) approaches to security valuation fail to provide the research analyst with any *direct* information on how the firm's current and future investment opportunities determine the market value of the firm and its outstanding debt and equity securities.

Unlike EVA, earnings-based models can result in the misestimation of a firm's market value and outstanding shares because of potential accounting distortions in the "bottom-line" earnings-per-share (EPS) measure. Moreover, the innovative EVA model can be used to estimate the market value of growth-oriented companies in sectors like technology where traditional DDM procedures are irrelevant — because of a dearth of dividend information — and price-relative approaches to equity valuation can yield volatile results.

THE EVA APPROACH TO CORPORATE VALUATION

Although the traditional DDMs are often difficult to use in practice, they do provide some meaningful insight into developing alternative EVA-growth approaches to corporate valuation. To begin, it was shown in Chapter 2 that the market value of the firm is equal to the initial capital investment *plus* the present value of the anticipated EVA stream that is generated on the firm's assets. This latter term is of course the firm's *total* market value-added (MVA, or aggregate NPV) at time period zero.

---

[1] See Eugene F. Fama and Merton H. Miller, *The Theory of Finance* (Holt, Rinehart, and Winston 1972).

From a corporate valuation perspective, these EVA-based concepts can be modeled as:

$$V(0) = C(0) + MVA(0)$$
$$= C(0) + \Sigma \, EVA(t)/(1 + COC)^t$$
$$= C(0) + \Sigma \, [C_{t-1}(RROC)]/(1 + COC)^t$$

where

C(0)	=	the firm's total capital employed in the business
MVA(0)	=	the firm's aggregate market value-added at period zero
RROC	=	the "residual (or surplus) return" earned on the capital in place at $t-1$

The EVA(t) term in the above expression is the economic value added at (t) expected on the firm's real assets in place at time period ($t-1$). This corporate profit metric derives its value from the product of the firm's expected residual (or surplus) return on capital (RROC) and the corresponding beginning-of-year capital stock (C_{t-1}). Also, unless otherwise noted in the valuation expressions that follow, the "Σ" sign runs from $t = 1$ to ∞.

The Constant Growth EVA Model

If, for simplicity, one assumes that the firm's expected EVA is growing at some long-term (constant) rate of growth, say, g_{LT}, each year forever, then one obtains the familiar "Gordon-like" EVA-growth model:

$$V(0) = C(0) + MVA(0)$$
$$= C(0) + EVA(1)/(COC - g_{LT})$$

where

EVA(1)	=	the assessed economic value added from the firm's existing assets
g_{LT}	=	the expected long-term EVA growth rate that is largely generated by the company's future assets not currently in place at time period zero.

The constant growth version of the general EVA model was used in Chapter 2 to show the pricing impact of NSF's opportunity to generate economic value added for the future. In this basic pricing illustration, the firm's *overall* market value can be expressed as:

$$V(0) = \$100 + MVA(0)$$
$$= \$100 + \$15/(0.1 - 0.025)$$
$$= \$300 \text{ million}$$

Additionally, with $100 million in long-term debt and 10 million common shares, the intrinsic worth of NSF's stock is $20 per share.

From a more dynamic perspective, the constant growth model reveals that the firm's net present value is positively related to both the near-term EVA outlook and the firm's long-term EVA growth rate (g_{LT}). On the other hand, a simultaneous rise in the firm's cost of capital — due to higher interest rates or a rise in the economy-wide business risk premium — can have a negative impact on the market value added from the firm's future growth opportunities. The best of both pricing scenarios happens when the firm's weighted average cost of capital falls — due perhaps to a fall in interest rates, or a decrease in the firm's *unlevered* risk premium — in the presence of an unanticipated rise in the firm's long-term EVA growth rate, (g_{LT}).[2]

The Variable Growth EVA Model

Since the firm's economic growth largely varies over time, the constant growth model has some obvious practical limitations. In particular, this version of the general EVA model requires that the growth rate in the firm's economic value-added not only be constant for all future time periods, but also that it be consistently *below* the firm's weighted average cost of capital (COC). This mature growth condition is clearly inconsistent with the corporate profit experiences of many growth-oriented firms that operate in economic sectors such as beverages, computer software and services, and semiconductors.

Fortunately, the firm's pricing precision can be improved by recognizing that the general EVA model can be unfolded into multiple stages of economic growth. For instance, in the two-stage version of this model — abnormal EVA growth followed by mature growth to infinity — the firm's market value-added (MVA) can be expressed in present value terms as:

$$MVA(0) = \Sigma^T EVA(t)/(1 + COC)^t + PVIF_{COC,T} [MVA(T)]$$
$$= \Sigma^T [......] + PVIF_{COC,T} [EVA(T+1)/(COC-g_{LT})]$$

The first term on the right hand side of the two-stage pricing model is the intrinsic value of the firm's expected EVA during the near-term growth phase. During these abnormal years, the firm's EVA is growing at the unusually high (or low) rate of g_{NT}. However, because of competition and/or technological considerations within the industry, the growth rate in the firm's economic value-added settles down to g_{LT} for the long term. In this context, the MVA(T) term in the valuation expression represents the firm's market value added at the *termination* of the firm's abnormal EVA growth phase.

---

[2] This condition of rising capital returns in the presence of falling capital costs is consistent with the experience of the U.S. economy in the post-1991 years (through 1995). For more on this economy-wide EVA occurrence, see Chapter 10.

Hence, the second term in the two-stage variable growth model reveals that the firm derives its market value added at T from the anticipated EVA at period $T+1$, discounted back to that time by the long-term EVA "capitalization rate" (COC − g_{LT}). The present value interest factor (pvif = $1/(1 + COC)^T$) is then used to discount the firm's expected market value added at T, back to the current time period (zero). Upon adding the two EVA-based pricing expressions to the firm's current capital investment (C(0)), one obtains the aggregate value of the firm (V(0)).

A NUMERICAL ILLUSTRATION OF THE VARIABLE GROWTH EVA MODEL

As a numerical illustration of the two-stage variable growth model, suppose that the firm's EVA at period 1 is expected to grow at the near-term rate of 10% for three years. Following this abnormal growth phase (where g_{NT} equals COC) the firm's EVA growth rate is expected to fall back to the 2.5% rate used in the constant growth example. Exhibit 1 shows how the firm's market value-added at period *zero* can be estimated in the context of a convenient pricing *template* for the two-stage EVA growth model.

Combining the MVA Results from Steps A and B:

The pricing template (Exhibit 1) reveals that the firm's *total* net present value is the sum of the market value added from the near-term (abnormal) EVA growth opportunity and the MVA contribution from the firm's long-term (mature) economic growth strategy. Upon adding the financial results shown here, the two-step procedure yields the firm's aggregate market value added at time period zero:

$$MVA(0) = \textit{Step A plus Step B}$$
$$= \$54.56 + \$186.41$$
$$= \$240.97$$

At \$340.97 million, the firm's overall market value, V(0), is the sum of the total capital employed in the business and its aggregate net present value as measured in the exhibit by MVA(0). This corporate valuation development can be expressed as:

$$V(0) = C(0) + MVA(0)$$
$$= \$100 + \$240.97$$
$$= \$340.97$$

Upon subtracting the (assumed) \$100 million in long-term debt from the firm's estimated market value, the firm's total equity capitalization, \$240.97 million, is obtained. With 10 million common shares outstanding, the intrinsic (present) value of the stock is \$24.10. Hence, the near-term EVA growth opportunity leads to a 20% (\$4.10/\$20) improvement in the company's stock price when compared to the valuation result obtained in the constant growth model.

Exhibit 1: Pricing Template for the Two-Stage EVA Growth Model

Step A: Calculate the MVA contribution from the estimated EVA stream during the *abnormal* growth phase. This portion of the pricing template shows the estimated EVA figures for years 1 through 4, along with their present values when discounted at the 10% cost of capital.

Market Value Added from the Firm's Near-Term EVA Growth Opportunity (in $ millions)

Period	0	1	2	3	4*
EVA(t)	—	15	16.50	18.15	19.97
$PVIF_{10,t} \times EVA(t)$		13.64	13.64	13.64	13.64
*$EVA(t) = EVA(t-1) [1 + g_{NT}]$, for $t = 2$ to 4					

MVA(0) from Near-Term Growth
Opportunity: $54.56 = \Sigma^4 \, EVA(t)/(1.1)^t$

Step B: Calculate the MVA contribution from the estimated EVA stream generated during the *mature* growth phase. This section of the pricing template shows how to calculate the present value at period zero (now) of the firm's estimated Market Value Added at time period *T*.

Market Value-Added from the Firm's Long-Term Growth Opportunities (in $ millions)

$$
\begin{aligned}
EVA(5) &= EVA(4)[1 + g_{LT}] \\
&= \$19.97 \, (1.025) \\
&= \$20.47 \\
MVA(4) &= EVA(5)/(COC - g_{LT}) \\
&= \$20.47/(0.10 - 0.025) \\
&= \$272.93
\end{aligned}
$$

MVA(0) from Long-Term
Growth Opportunities
$$
\begin{aligned}
&= PVIF_{10,4} \times MVA(4) \\
&= 0.683 \times \$272.93 \\
&= \$186.41
\end{aligned}
$$

In light of the EVA-based models presented so far, it should be apparent that the firm derives it total net present value (NPV) from both the near-term EVA outlook and the long-term forecast on this measure of real corporate profitability. With these valuation developments in mind, it is possible to see why some wealth creators can have positive market value added (MVA) in the presence of their currently negative EVA outlook. In a pricing nutshell, investors are largely optimistic about the firm's *long-term* ability to generate economic value added for the future.

Moreover, in the selected instances of wealth destroyers with a currently favorable EVA outlook — Chrysler and Ford Motor Company, as presented in Chapter 5 —the efficient market argument implies that investors were exceedingly *pessimistic* about the EVA outlook for these automakers over the long haul. If this were not the case, then the debt and equity securities of the so-called "wealth destroyers" with a currently-positive EVA outlook would be undervalued in the marketplace. That is, Chrysler Corporation in particular would have been a "buy opportunity" at that time.

VALUATION LINKS WITH THE CLASSIC NPV MODEL

The wealth implications of the variable growth EVA model can also be illustrated in the context of the two-period NPV model described in Chapter 2. In this context, it is important to recognize that the firm's *residual cash flow* (RCF) in the forthcoming year is a reflection of (1) the intrinsic value at period 1 of the company's near-term EVA stream and (2) the present value of the long-term EVA growth opportunities when discounted back to that time.

For ease of calculation, it is helpful to recognize that the firm's anticipated RCF at Period 1 can also be estimated in terms of the market value added (MVA) at time period zero and the product of (one plus) the weighted average cost of capital. At $265.07 million, the firm's residual cash flow (RCF) can be conveniently estimated according to:

$$RCF(1) = \Sigma^T EVA(t)/(1 + COC)^{t-1} + PVIF_{COC,T-1} [MVA(T)]$$
$$= [MVA(0)] (1 + COC)$$
$$= [240.97] (1.1)$$
$$= \$265.07$$

Upon inserting the estimated RCF(1) and MVA(0) figures into the NPV graph shown in Exhibit 2, one obtains the desired graphical results. In particular, the classic NPV model shows that the firm's aggregate market value added is equal to the intrinsic value of the anticipated residual cash flow. The firm's RCF at year 1 (MVA(1)) is equal to the discounted value at that time of the firm's near-term EVA outlook, $60 million, *plus* the assessed valuation (at period 1) of its long-term ability to generate economic value added, $205 million.

Exhibit 2: NPV Illustration of the Variable Growth EVA Model

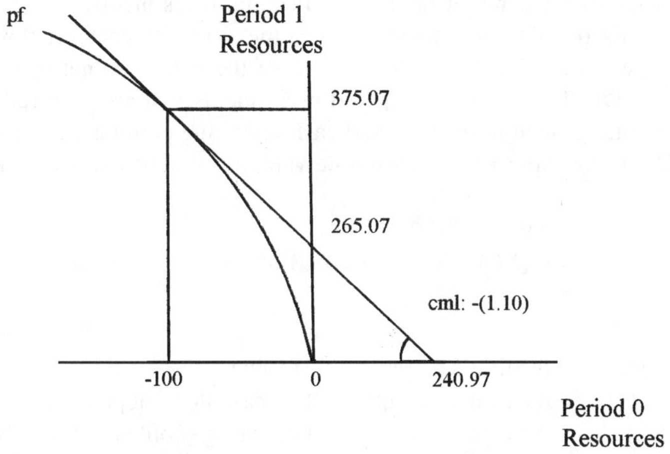

At \$375.07 million, the two-period NPV illustration also shows the firm's estimated market value at time period 1. The company's overall intrinsic worth at this time is obtained by growing its current estimated value, \$340.97 million, at the 10% expected capital cost for one year. By extension, the two-period (NPV) wealth findings shown in Exhibit 2 suggests that EVA is a theoretically-robust financial metric in any multi-period framework.

EVA AND CORPORATE VALUATION: ADVANCED CONSIDERATIONS

As mentioned before, there are many equivalent ways of estimating the intrinsic value of the firm and its outstanding shares. Two of the more pertinent valuation approaches in this book include the Free Cash Flow (FCF) model and the Investment Opportunities Approach to Corporate Valuation. As demonstrated by Fama and Miller, these corporate valuation models focus directly on the economic source of the firm's market capitalization. Their IOAV model can be used to emphasize the EVA-importance of the firm's existing *and* anticipated future assets (not currently in place) in determining the firm's market valuation.

The Free Cash Flow Approach to Corporate Valuation

One of the benefits of the Free Cash Flow approach to corporate valuation is that it recognizes that the firm's revenue and earnings growth cannot be sustained without any *future* investment in real capital. Rather than saying simply that the firm derives its market value from the discounted future earnings stream, this model looks at corporate valuation in terms of the intrinsic worth of the anticipated "net cash flows" — that is, the discounted value of the expected after-tax cash operating earnings net of the required capital investments.

In this popular investment model, the firm's "free cash flow" for any given time period can be expressed in terms of the *unlevered* net operating profit after tax (UNOPAT) and the anticipated investments that are required to support the fundamental growth in revenue and cash operating earnings. In general terms, the Free Cash Flow approach to corporate valuation can be expressed as:

$$V(0) = \Sigma \; FCF(t)/(1 + COC)^t$$
$$= \Sigma \; [X(t) - I(t)]/(1 + COC)^t$$

where

V(0)	=	the firm's current market value
FCF(t)	=	the firm's anticipated "free cash flow" at period t
X(t)	=	the firm's unlevered net operating profit after tax (UNOPAT)
COC	=	the weighted average cost of capital

As a modeling convenience, it is generally assumed that the firm's free cash flow is growing at an abnormal rate for T periods (five or ten years). After the initial growth phase, it is assumed that the firm's future assets generate a perpetuity in the amount of $X(T)$ each year, forever. The UNOPAT then has a market value at T of $X(T)/COC$. Some insightful illustrations of the variable growth approach to implementing the Free Cash Flow model are covered in the acquisitions literature by Alfred Rappaport,[3] and the recent FCF versus EVA model comparisons provided by Al Jackson, Michael J. Mauboussin, and Charles R. Wolf.[4]

The Investment Opportunities Approach (IOAV) to Corporate Valuation

Although the Free Cash Flow approach to corporate valuation is a step in the right direction, the model in its general form doesn't make an *explicit* connection between the firm's future after-tax cash flow and its underlying NPV. However, with some simplifying assumptions, Fama and Miller show that the FCF model can be unfolded into two EVA-related pricing components.[5]

---

[3] An interesting application of the FCF model in evaluating corporate acquisition candidates can be found in Alfred Rappaport, "Strategic Analysis for More Profitable Acquisitions," *Harvard Business Review* (July/August 1979).

[4] For a comparison of the FCF- versus EVA-model, see Al Jackson, Michael J. Mauboussin, and Charles R. Wolf, "EVA® Primer," *Equity Research-Americas* (CS First Boston: February 20, 1996).

[5] It is important to mention that Fama and Miller do not express their corporate valuation ideas in the MVA and EVA jargon of Stern-Stewart. However, the IOAV model — as explained in *The Theory of Finance* — should be recognized as providing solid academic support for the EVA approach to corporate valuation. This point is also recognized by Joel Stern and Bennett Stewart III, through their references to Merton H. Miller and Franco Modigliani, "Dividend Policy, Growth, and the Valuation of Shares," *Journal of Business* (October 1961).

In particular, Fama and Miller show that the firm's market value can be expressed in terms of the intrinsic worth of the expected net operating cash flow stream (X(1)) that is generated by the firm's existing assets and the market value of the firm's anticipated future growth opportunities (G). In this powerful investment model, the firm's market capitalization can be expressed as:

$$V(0) = X(1)/COC + \Sigma\ I(t)[RROC(t)/COC]/(1 + COC)^t$$
$$= X(1)/COC + G\ [I(t), RROC(t)]$$

where

V(0)	=	the firm's current value
X(1)	=	the expected (perpetual) net operating cash flow generated by the firm's existing assets
I(t)	=	the firm's *future* investment in real assets at period t
RROC(t)	=	the firm's assessed "residual return" on the future capital additions at (t)

Σ runs from $t = 1$ to ∞

The IOAV approach to corporate valuation separates the market value of the firm into two major components. The first term on the right-hand side of the expression is the present value of the *unlevered* net operating cash flow (X(1)) generated by the firm's existing assets. The second, and more complex-looking, term on the right hand side of the IOAV equation is the market value of the firm's expected future growth opportunities (G). As shown, this pricing term is related to the capital additions at t, and the assessed residual rate of return (RROC(t)) on the firm's perceived future growth opportunities.

In the IOAV model, the firm's investment opportunities make a value-added contribution to its current value when the anticipated return on these capital additions exceeds the weighted average COC. On the other hand, when the after tax capital return is less than the assessed cost of capital, the market value of the firm falls currently, when, for instance, corporate managers expand the real asset base for reasons that are inconsistent with the principles of wealth maximization. Hence, in this investment model, the present value of the firm's future growth opportunities (G) is *positive* when the assessed "residual return" on the future investments (RROC(t)) is largely positive.

It is now possible to make a formal connection between the classic IOAV model and the innovative EVA measure. Based on the conventional definition of this financial metric, it is possible to express the firm's expected EVA on the future capital investments as:

$$eva\ (t+1) = I(t)ROC(t) - I(t)COC$$
$$= I(t)[ROC(t) - COC]$$
$$= I(t)[RROC(t)]$$

where

$I(t)ROC(t)$ = the firm's expected after-tax operating cash flow at period $t+1$ on the capital additions

$I(t)COC$ = the firm's expected dollar cost of capital (at $t+1$) on these future investment opportunities.

By substituting $eva(t+1)$ for the $I(t)[ROC(t) - COC]$ term in the IOAV model, we obtain:

$$V(0) = X(1)/COC + \Sigma[eva\ (t+1)/COC]/(1 + COC)^t$$

This expression clearly indicates that the firm's valuation is ultimately linked to the ability of its managers to invest in growth opportunities having a measure of "economic value added." In this context, the market value of the firm's future growth opportunities (G) is based on shareholders' perceptions of the firm's underlying ability to generate EVA for the future. As expected, these growth opportunities make a positive contribution to the firm's intrinsic value when the anticipated after-tax return on invested capital $(ROC(t))$ exceeds on the average the firm's expected cost of capital (COC).

Moreover, the discounted EVA perpetuity in the brackets, $[eva\ (t+1)/\ COC]$, is the "market value added $[mva\ (t)]$" from the firm's real investment opportunity at time t. This present value interpretation reveals that G is in effect the "market value added" at time zero from *all* of the firm's expected future growth opportunities. With this development, the market value of the firm can be expressed as:[6]

$$V(0) = X(1)/COC + \Sigma\ [mva(t)]/(1 + COC)^t$$

IOAV and EVA: A Closer Look at the Present Value Linkage

A simple rearrangement of the classic IOAV model reveals that the firm's total market value $(V(0))$ can be expressed as the firm's initial capital investment *plus* the present value of the anticipated EVA stream generated by both existing assets and

---

[6] $V(0)$ represents the market value of the *unlevered* firm having growth opportunities where the residual return on future capital is positive (for some periods). If corporate debt policy is irrelevant as Miller and Modigliani contend, then $V(0)$ also represents the aggregate value of the *levered* firm. Otherwise, the unlevered and levered firms differ in corporate pricing terms by the present value of the effective debt tax subsidy received on the levered shares.

There are of course some helpful *finite* representations of the generalized IOAV model. For instance, in *The Quest for Value*, Stewart describes the market value of the unlevered firm with a "forward plan (or positive growth opportunity)," as:

$$V(0) = X(1)/COC + [I(RROC)T]/\ COC(1+COC),$$

where (using the notation that corresponds with this book) $X(1)$ is the unlevered net operating profit after tax, COC is the familiar cost of capital, I is the normal future yearly investment in real assets, and T is the finite duration over which the firm can expand with a *positive* residual return on capital {that is, [RROC=ROC-COC]>0}. Jackson, Mauboussin, and Wolf use this finite version of the IOAV model in their EVA growth illustrations, see, "EVA® Primer."

expected capital assets. To show this link to present value, it is helpful to recognize that the firm's net operating cash flow perpetuity ($X(1)$) can be modeled as:

$$X(1) = COC \times C(0) + EVA(1)$$

where the product of the firm's cost of capital (COC) and its initial capital investment ($C(0)$) equals the *dollar* capital cost on the firm's existing assets, and the $EVA(1)$ term is the firm's anticipated economic value added at period 1. Substituting this expression for $X(1)$ into the first term on the right hand side of the IOAV model yields:

$$
\begin{aligned}
V(0) &= X(1)/COC + G(I(t), RROC(t)) \\
&= C(0) + [EVA(1)/ COC + G(.)] \\
&= C(0) + MVA(0)
\end{aligned}
$$

In this context, the IOAV-EVA link gives a powerful representation of the market value of the firm. The linked model suggests that the firm derives its market value added (MVA) from the present value of the EVA stream that is expected from assets already in place as well as the likely capital investments for the future. Thus, the firm's total net present value is obtained by summing the two MVA-based pricing terms shown within the brackets.

In the previous equation, the $EVA(1)/COC$ term represents the MVA contribution that is being generated by the firm's existing assets and the $G[I(t), RROC(t)]$ function represents the net present value of the firm's anticipated future growth opportunities. Taken together, the two sources of economic value added — EVA from both current and anticipated future real assets — represent the firm's total MVA at time period zero.

The IOAV-EVA link provides some meaningful insight for both wealth creators and destroyers. The model demonstrates that the firm's market value added is positive only if the expected after-tax return on the future real investments exceeds the *cross-generational* COC. The opposite MVA prediction would apply for wealth destroyers having a largely negative expected residual return on investment for the future.

SUMMARY

This chapter shows how to use the EVA metric to calculate the intrinsic value of the firm. In principle, the firm's MVA is equal to the present value of the anticipated EVA stream for all future time periods. From this perspective it is possible to develop a series of practitioner-oriented models that use the EVA measure to estimate the market value of the firm and its outstanding shares. Some helpful pricing variations on the general EVA model include the constant growth version and the two-stage EVA growth model. Multiple stages of growth in the firm's real corporate profitability can be added should the valuation need arise.

In the constant growth EVA model, the firm's MVA is expressed in terms of the current EVA outlook (as measured by EVA(1)) and the company's assessed long-term EVA growth rate (g_{LT}). The model suggests that companies having positive EVA growth expectations (at some assumed constant rate for all future time periods) should see noticeable improvements in the market value of the firm and its outstanding securities. In effect, the positive EVA growth increases the stockholder's residual claim on the firm's expected profits, while the "good news" about the firm's anticipated economic value added may also lead to credit upgrades in its outstanding bonds.

The variable-growth EVA model is a more realistic way of seeing how the firm derives its real corporate profitability. In the two-stage version of the model, the firm's total market value added (MVA) is separated into the sum of (1) the present value of the EVA stream generated during the firm's abnormal growth phase and (2) the intrinsic worth of the expected EVA benefits generated during the long-term (mature) growth period. The total of these MVA-related pricing elements is the firm's total net present value. Moreover, with estimates of four identifiable parameters — including EVA(1), g_{NT}, g_{LT}, and COC — the two stage EVA pricing template can be used in practice by corporate managers and investors.

The benefit of using the EVA metric to estimate the firm's market value does not lie in its ability to produce a theoretically better estimate of the present value of the firm and its outstanding shares. The "franchise value" of any company is derived from the intrinsic worth of the real economic benefits — whether they be measured in terms of dividends per share, free cash flow, or even EVA — generated by the firm's capital assets (both human and physical). This is one of the central valuation themes in financial economics. It is also one of the major reasons why the firm's "capital structure" decision is largely irrelevant for firms operating in a well-functioning capital market.

Rather, the real benefit of using EVA technology to value companies is based on three important considerations. Since EVA is the *annualized* equivalent of the firm's total net present value, this metric makes a tangible connection with the economist's view of how wealth is truly created in an efficient capital market. This corporate valuation point is most directly emphasized in the "Investment Opportunities Approach to Valuation (IOAV)" where the firm derives its aggregate MVA from the anticipated EVA stream on both existing assets and future capital additions not currently in place. These human and physical assets make a meaningful contribution to the firm's net present value when the assessed residual return on capital, RROC(t), exceeds the cross-generational cost of capital.

In addition, the EVA-based pricing technique is quite versatile because it can be used to value companies in a variety of real world settings. Unlike the traditional dividend discount models, the variable-growth EVA model can be used to value companies that operate in the more growth-oriented sectors of the economy, where, in many instances, corporate plowback ratios are near unity. Since the EVA metric looks at how the firm generates its overall corporate profitability, the derived pricing models have several joint investment implications for the firm's outstanding equity *and* debt securities.

Chapter 7

Estimating MVA with Published Financial Reports

The EVA approach to corporate valuation makes an *explicit* connection with how wealth is truly created in an efficient capital market. This pricing benefit happens because the intrinsic worth of the anticipated EVA stream produces a meaningful estimate of the firm's *net present value*. Managerial decisions (through internal growth opportunities or corporate acquisitions) that enhance the firm's market value added (MVA) lead to an increase in shareholder wealth, while corporate actions that cause negative net present value results actually destroy it. Unfortunately, the published data that investors and managers may use to calculate the firm's market value added is rarely in a form that is conducive to making the EVA valuation approach a simple task.

In particular, the two-step procedure (pricing template) used to calculate the firm's net present value seems easy enough if one has in hand the relevant EVA estimates. In practice, though, the *four* key parameters of the variable growth model — including EVA(1), g_{NT}, g_{LT}, and COC — need to be estimated from financial reports that may look challenging to both managers and investors when viewed in an EVA context. In an attempt to illustrate — and hopefully overcome — some of the "real world" measurement difficulties that may arise, let's take a look at a recent Value Line report to see how published data can be used to energize the variable growth EVA model.

ESTIMATING EVA WITH PUBLISHED FINANCIAL REPORTS: THE CASE OF AMERICAN HOME PRODUCTS CORPORATION

Exhibit 1 shows the August 2, 1996 Value Line report for American Home Products (AHP) Corporation. As shown, the published financial report does not provide any direct EVA information that can be used to estimate the firm's market value added. Specifically, the *unlevered* net operating profit after taxes (UNOPAT) and the (dollar) weighted average cost of capital figures are absent from the company report. These data omissions represent the two major items that are used to calculate the firm's economic value added for any given year. Likewise, without the weighted average cost of capital (COC) there is no direct way of estimating the residual return on capital (RROC) for this well-known drug firm.

Exhibit 1: Value Line Report for American Home Products Corporation

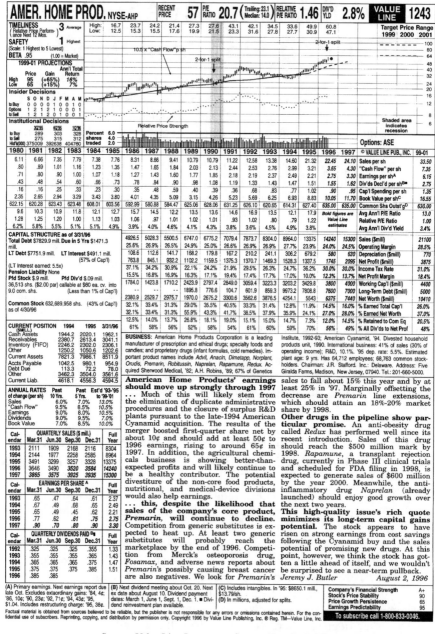

Source: Value Line Investment Survey, New York, NY.

A closer look at the Value Line report for American Home Products Corporation reveals that it does provide many subsidiary metrics for calculating key components of the firm's "ex ante" EVA. The published report lists, by year, the anticipated sales, the operating profit margin (OPM), the depreciation amount, and the estimated income tax rate. These yearly financial estimates can be "rolled up" into the firm's UNOPAT.

Likewise, the research report provides some helpful information for interpreting AHP's weighted average COC. The report includes information that can be used to assess the pre-tax cost of debt and the potential "target debt weight" in the firm's capital structure. Also, the Value Line "beta coefficient" can be used as the *relative* risk input when calculating the firm's (CAPM) cost of equity capital. With this background, we can see how the Value Line report can be used to estimate the major components of the two-stage EVA growth model.

The research focus can now turn to how the reported data can be used to calculate the market value added (MVA) for American Home Products Corporation. This corporate valuation illustration will be examined in the context of (1) AHP's EVA forecast for 1997, (2) the near-term and long-term EVA growth rates, and (3) the firm's weighted average cost of debt and equity capital. Based on the Value Line presentation format, it is assumed that the market value of the firm and its outstanding shares are being evaluated at year-end 1996.

The One-Step Ahead EVA Estimate

One of the helpful inputs to the two-stage EVA growth model is the firm's estimated economic value added for the forthcoming year. This *one-step ahead* EVA forecast is important in the model because it can be combined with knowledge of the near-term EVA growth rate, g_{NT}, to provide company estimates of the EVA stream during the abnormal growth period. Since Value Line does not provide any EVA estimates, this figure will have to be inferred from the financial information provided in their research report.

The first component of the one-step-ahead EVA forecast is the firm's UNOPAT. In general terms this part of the firm's economic value added for any given year can be expressed as:

$$UNOPAT = EBITD(1 - t) + tD_p$$

where

$EBITD$ = the firm's estimated earnings before interest and taxes (EBIT) and depreciation

tD_p = the estimated depreciation tax subsidy

A quick look at Exhibit 1 reveals that Value Line does not list the yearly EBIT or EBITD figures. However, AHP's estimated earnings before interest and taxes (EBIT) for 1997 can be calculated by multiplying the estimated sales figure, $15.3 billion, by the corresponding operating margin, 24.5%. Upon adding the

1997 depreciation figure, $0.63 billion, to this product, we obtain the firm's anticipated EBITD value for 1997:

$$\begin{aligned} \text{EBITD}(1997) &= \text{EBIT} + D_p \\ &= [\text{Sales} \times \text{OPM}] + D_p \\ &= [\$15.3 \times 0.245] + \$0.63 \\ &= [\$3.749] + \$0.63 \\ &= \$4.379 \text{ billion} \end{aligned}$$

Once the 1997 EBITD figure and the estimated tax rate, 30%, are known, it is possible to calculate the *one-step ahead* forecast of AHP's unlevered net operating profit after tax:

$$\begin{aligned} \text{UNOPAT}(1997) &= \text{EBITD} \, (1 - t) + tD_p \\ &= \$4.379 \, (1 - 0.3) + 0.3(\$0.63) \\ &= \$3.065 + \$0.189 \\ &= \$3.254 \text{ billion} \end{aligned}$$

Estimating the Cost of Capital for American Home Products Corporation

The second essential ingredient in the production of the firm's 1997 EVA estimate is the *dollar* cost of capital. In order to assess AHP's forthcoming capital cost, one needs to know something about (1) the company's after-tax cost of debt financing, (2) the required return on the common equity, and (3) the firm's "target debt weight" (if any) in the corporate capital structure.

AHP's pre-tax cost of debt financing can be estimated by using the information provided in the "Capital Structure Box" on the Value Line report. The firm's pre-tax debt rate, 6.335%, is obtained by dividing the long term interest expense, $0.4911 billion, by the long term debt figure, $7.7519 billion. This pre-tax rate can then be "tax-adjusted" by 30% to produce an after-tax gauge of the firm's "ex ante" cost of debt financing for 1997. These calculations result in a post-tax cost of debt financing for American Home Products of 4.435%.

The Cost of Equity Capital for American Home Products Corporation

AHP's cost of equity capital can now be estimated according to the capital asset pricing model. In this context, the firm's required equity return is obtained with knowledge of the risk-free rate of interest, the anticipated market risk premium, and the "systematic risk," or beta sensitivity, of the common stock. With a risk-free rate of 7% (at that time), a "market risk premium" of 6%, and a Value Line beta sensitivity of 0.95, AHP's cost of equity is calculated as follows:

$$\begin{aligned} \text{CAPM} &= R_f + \text{MRP} \times \text{Beta} \\ &= 7\% + 6\% \times 0.95 \\ &= 12.7\% \end{aligned}$$

Thus, in a CAPM context, the stockholders at American Home Products are looking for the firm's managers to generate a 12.7% return on their equity capital.This expected return figure is slightly below the 13% rate that would be required on the equity of the average firm in the marketplace. This happens because AHP's stock beta lies below the "market beta," which, by definition, is unity. (For convenience, the small amount of preferred stock in AHP's capital structure is treated like the common equity).

A Look at AHP's Corporate Debt Policy

If corporate debt policy (due to capital market imperfections) matters in the real world, then one needs to know something meaningful about the firm's "target debt weight" in the capital structure. For American Home Products Corporation, the "just right" amount of financial leverage has been particularly elusive over the years. In this context, the Value Line report shows that the level of corporate debt at this drug company has been particularly volatile during the reporting years.

For instance, the published report shows that American Home Products Corporation was 100% equity financed in the years listed before 1989. During the 1989 to 1991 period, the long-term debt experience at this firm was highly volatile, ranging from 49% of "book capital" down to 3.1% at year-end 1991. Then, in the aftermath of AHP's corporate acquisition program (Genetics Institute (1992-1993), and American Cyanamid (1994), in particular), the firm's long-term debt soared to 58.5% of total capital by year-end 1995.

As a result of this historical volatility, the issue of a meaningful target debt level for American Home Products Corporation is a problematic one. Assuming that AHP has an "optimal capital structure," then one way of estimating the firm's target debt ratio is to use the forward-looking (ex ante) long-term debt and net worth (equity) figures provided on the Value Line report. In this context, the published report shows that long-term debt makes up approximately *one-third* of the estimated "book capital" (long-term debt plus net worth) from 1999 to 2001. If correct, then AHP's *ex-ante* percentage of long-term debt relative to the *futuristic* capital employed in the business can be used as a reasonable estimate of the "target debt weight" in the firm's cost of capital calculation.

Combining the Capital Cost Inputs for American Home Products Corporation

The overall percentage cost of capital for AHP is a weighted average of the post-tax cost of debt and equity capital. The firm's estimated 1997 cost of capital is calculated as follows:

$$COC = w_d \times r_{d,at} + w_e \times r_e$$
$$= (1/3) \times 4.435\% + (2/3) \times 12.7\%$$
$$= 9.945\%$$

where

w_d = the target debt weight
$r_{d,at}$ = the after-tax cost of debt
r_e = the expected return on the stock

This COC percentage represents the corporate-wide "discount rate" for American Home Products Corporation. It will be used shortly as the *overall* required return for AHP in the calculation of its MVA.

By multiplying the estimated 1996 book capital (long-term debt plus net worth) for American Home Products by the weighted average COC, we obtain the firm's estimated *dollar* capital cost for 1997:

$$\$ \text{Cost of Capital}(1997) = C(1996) \times [\text{COC}/100]$$
$$= \$13.975 \times [9.945/100]$$
$$= \$1.39 \text{ billion}$$

As with the UNOPAT measure, this dollar cost of capital figure is needed to calculate AHP's economic value added for 1997 and beyond.

AHP's Near-Term Expected EVA Stream

With this foundation, the *one-step ahead* EVA forecast for AHP is now obtained by subtracting the estimated dollar cost of capital from the UNOPAT. Combining the relevant financial inputs yields AHP's estimated EVA for 1997:

$$\$\text{EVA}(1997) = \text{UNOPAT}(1997) - \$ \text{COC}(1997)$$
$$= \$3.254 - \$1.39$$
$$= \$1.864 \text{ billion.}$$

This development is important not only because it produces the forecast EVA figure for 1997, but also because the same procedure can be used to calculate AHP's (four-step ahead) EVA at the millennium. With the two EVA estimates separated by time, it is possible to calculate the *implied* near-term EVA growth rate, g_{NT}, during the 3-year period from (year-end) 1997 to 2000. The resulting near-term EVA growth rate can then be used to find the implied EVA estimates for 1998 and 1999. However, in order to estimate AHP's EVA for year-end 2000, one needs to have the firm's estimated total capital at year-end 1999. This book capital estimate (long-term debt plus net worth) is necessary because the dollar cost of capital for any given year is based on the beginning of year capital stock.

Fortunately, the implied book capital figure for American Home Products Corporation can be estimated with knowledge of the assessed growth rate in the firm's capital over the 4-year reporting period spanning 1996 to 2000. At 2.474%, the near-term capital growth rate, NTCGR, for this drug company during this 4-year time interval is calculated according to:

$$\text{NTCGR} = [15.41/13.975]^{0.25} - 1.0$$
$$= 1.02474 - 1.0$$
$$= 0.02474$$

Upon growing AHP's 1996 total capital estimate, \$13.975 billion, by the near-term capital growth rate, 2.474%, we then obtain an estimate of the firm's capital stock at year-end 1999:

$$C(1999) = C(1996) \times (1 + \text{NTCGR})^{3.0}$$
$$= 13.975 \times (1.02474)^3$$
$$= \$15.038 \text{ billion}$$

Moreover, upon interpreting the Value Line report for AHP in the same way we did to estimate the firm's EVA for 1997, we find that: (1) the estimated dollar cost of capital at year-end 2000 is \$1.496 billion, (2) the unlevered net operating profit after tax (UNOPAT) estimate is \$4.919 billion, and (3) the anticipated EVA for this large drug firm at the millennium is \$3.423 billion. Also, at 22.456%, the *implied* near-term EVA growth rate for American Home Products Corporation over the three-year period covering 1997 to 2000 can be used to assess the firm's economic value-added for the missing years — specifically, 1998 and 1999 — where financial data is absent from the Value Line report.

ESTIMATING MVA FROM PUBLISHED FINANCIAL REPORTS: THE CASE OF AMERICAN HOME PRODUCTS CORPORATION

It is now time to calculate the MVA for American Home Products Corporation using the two-stage EVA growth model. This procedure requires the calculation of both the present value of the anticipated EVA stream during the near-term growth phase and the intrinsic worth the firm's long-term ability to generate EVA for the future. This latter valuation term is the intrinsic value of AHP's anticipated market value added, MVA(2000), at the *millennium*. The two-step MVA-pricing procedure for American Home Products Corporation is outlined in Exhibit 2.

Combining the Valuation Results for AHP

AHP's *total* market value added at time period zero is the sum of the MVA generated from the abnormal EVA growth opportunity and the MVA contribution from the firm's mature economic growth. Upon adding the two pricing terms for AHP, the variable-growth EVA analysis yields the aggregate market value added (or NPV) at time period zero:

$$\text{MVA}(0) = Step\ A \text{ plus } Step\ B$$
$$= \$8.029 + \$27.778$$
$$= \$35.807 \text{ billion}$$

Exhibit 2: Pricing Template to Estimate the Market Value Added for American Home Products Corporation

Step A: Calculate the MVA contribution at year-end 1996 from the estimated EVA stream during the abnormal growth phase: The following results show the estimated EVA figures for the years 1997 through 2000, along with their current values when discounted at the firm's 9.95% cost of capital. The *implied* near-term EVA growth rate, g_{NT}, used in these calculations is 22.456%.

Market Value Added from AHP's Near-Term Growth Opportunity (in $ Billions)

Year	1996	1997	1998*	1999*	2000
Model Period (t)	0	1	2	3	4
EVA(t)	—	1.864	2.283	2.795	3.423
PVIF$_{9.95,t}$ EVA(t)		1.695	1.888	2.103	2.342
		* *Implied* EVA(t) estimates,			
		at EVA(t–1)*(1 + g_{NT})			

MVA(0) from Near-Term Growth
Opportunity: $8.029 billion = Σ^4 EVA(t)/(1.0995)^t

Step B: Calculate AHP's MVA contribution at year-end 1996 from the estimated EVA stream generated during the mature growth phase. For convenience, the long-term EVA growth rate, g_{LT}, for this drug firm is based on the 1984 to 1994 EVA data listed in the 1995 Stern Stewart Performance report. The resulting MVA contribution from this second step represents the present value of the firm's anticipated market value added at year-end 2000.

Market Value Added from AHP's Long-Term Growth Opportunities (in $ Billions)

$$EVA(5) = EVA(4)[1 + g_{LT}]$$
$$= \$3.423(1.014)$$
$$= \$3.471 \text{ billion}$$
$$MVA(4) = EVA(5)/(COC - g_{LT})$$
$$= \$3.471/(0.0995 - 0.014)$$
$$= \$40.596 \text{ billion}$$

MVA(0) from Long-Term
Growth Opportunities   = PVIF$_{9.95,4}$ × MVA(4)
$$= \$27.778 \text{ billion}$$

In turn, this wealth creator's market value, V(0), consists of the sum of the total capital employed in the business and the aggregate market value-added:

$$V(0) = C(0) + MVA(0)$$
$$= 13.975 + 35.807$$
$$= 49.782$$

Additionally, with 0.63269 billion shares, and the $7.6 billion in long-term debt outstanding, the *intrinsic value* of AHP's stock at year-end 1996 is $66.67. This present value figure results from dividing the drug firm's (estimated) equity capitalization, $42.182 billion, by the number of shares of stock outstanding at that time.

Thus, the variable-growth EVA model reveals that the stock of American Home Products Corporation is poised for a significant capital gain. Based on the $57 stock price shown on the Value Line report, it appears that the firm's equity securities (aside from the time value of money difference between the report date and the year-end 1996 evaluation date) were undervalued in the marketplace by some 17% ($66.67/57 − 1.0). In this context, the Value Line "timeliness" rating of 3 seems too conservative for this *wealth-creating* (and low-volatility) drug company. Moreover, from a traditional perspective, the return on equity (ROE) estimates for AHP Corporation — at 28% and 37% for the years 1997 and 2000 — are supportive of this optimistic performance assessment.

SUMMARY

This chapter shows how to use published financial reports to estimate a firm's market value added. In this example, a Value Line report for American Home Products Corporation was used to illustrate some of the practical challenges faced by managers and investors alike when using EVA-based discounting technology. Although no simple task, the AHP case study reveals that the firm's future EVA stream — and therefore, its current market value added — can be estimated with real world financial information. With this MVA knowledge, it is possible to calculate the intrinsic value of the firm and its outstanding shares.

Since EVA requires that managers think like owners, it challenges them to look at financial data in new wealth-creating ways. Unfortunately, most published financial reports are not presented in a format that is consistent with how wealth is truly created in a well-functioning capital market. There is no direct reporting of the firm's *unlevered* net operating profit after taxes or the weighted average cost of (debt and equity) capital on most published reports. Specifically, the essential UNOPAT and dollar COC inputs are missing from the company reports. Without these yearly figures, it can be difficult to calculate the firm's market value added.

To overcome this reporting limitation, managers and investors need to recast the conventional company reports, like Value Line, in a way that emphasizes the firm's "residual" profitability — that is, in a way that focuses on the firm's after-tax return on capital net of the capital costs. In order to estimate a firm's UNOPAT, researchers need to look "higher up" on the income statement toward EBITD. Upon tax-adjusting this pre-tax operating profit measure, and adding in the depreciation tax subsidy, tD_p, one obtains the firm's UNOPAT for any given time period.

In turn, after subtracting the firm's yearly *dollar* cost of capital from the UNOPAT estimates yields the firm's expected economic value added. As shown in the pricing illustration for American Home Products Corporation, the EVA estimates can then be "discounted" back to the current period to produce (1) the firm's market value added, (2) the EVA-assessed value of the firm, and (3) the intrinsic value of the company's stock. The 1996 EVA-based pricing application for AHP revealed that the firm was undervalued in the marketplace by some 17%.

Chapter 8

Company Analysis Using EVA

Financial analysis is generally required to find the best companies in the marketplace. In the traditional "growth style" of investing, research analysts frequently look for companies having abnormally high product development and earnings-growth prospects. By focusing research efforts primarily on the earnings per share, "E," it is anticipated that the common stock price, "P," will eventually catch up — if, in fact, it hasn't already done so. In practice, the revealed growth portfolio mostly consists of the shares of companies having a relatively high price-to-earnings ratio, a high price-to-book value ratio, and a low dividend yield. Moreover, this "P & E" view of the traditional growth style of investing is the essence of the "bottom up" approach to portfolio management that was used so successfully by Peter Lynch of Fidelity Investments.[1]

In the popular "value style" of investing, the research focus is primarily on the firm's stock price rather than the recent growth rate in its per share earnings. The investment presumption is that the company's stock price has fallen too far and too fast in view of the firm's *future* earnings prospects and the economic quality of the assets employed in the business. In practice, the revealed value portfolio largely consists of the shares of companies having a comparatively low price-to-earnings ratio, a low price-to-book value ratio, and a relatively high dividend yield. Over time, it is anticipated that the debt and equity securities of these so-called "value-oriented" companies will appreciate to a level which is more consistent with the firm's true wealth-creating potential.

Indeed, the real world importance of finding "good companies" in the marketplace that are selling at attractive prices is no secret. A growing body of empirical research suggests that a value-focused investment strategy produces abnormally high risk-adjusted portfolio returns.[2] Studies by Eugene Fama and Kenneth French as well as Rex Sinquefield suggest that abnormal return performance from the value style of investing applies to both the domestic U.S. and the international securities markets.[3]

Although the conventional growth and value strategies emphasize to varying degrees the research importance of the "P" and the "E," there is a similarity

---

[1] Peter Lynch's recent view on the fundamental linkage between stock price and per-share earnings can be found in, "Mind Your P's and E's," *Worth* (February 1996). From an EVA perspective, this "P and E" relationship might now be interpreted as, "Mind Your MVA's and EVA's!"

[2] See James L. Grant, "A Yield Effect in Common Stock Return," *Journal of Portfolio Management* (Winter 1995).

[3] That "value wins" from an investment perspective is described in Eugene F. Fama and Kenneth R. French, "The Cross Section of Expected Stock Returns," *Journal of Finance* (June 1992) and Rex A. Sinquefield, "Where Are the Gains From International Diversification?" *Financial Analysts Journal* (January/February 1996).

between these active approaches to investment management. In each case, the over-all goal is to maximize the likelihood of financial success while minimizing the risk of paying *too much* for the shares of (apparently) mispriced firms. In the growth style, the investor tries to avoid paying excessive multiples for those companies having unrealistic product development and earnings-growth expectations. In the popular value strategy, the active investor shuns the debt and equity securities of companies that may look "cheap" in the marketplace, when, in fact, their low prices are an efficient market reflection of the firm's poor future growth opportunities.

TOWARDS AN EVA GROWTH STRATEGY

By analogy, a modern perspective on the "growth style" of investing should empha-size the positive EVA happenings at the firm. By focusing research efforts on those companies having abnormally high EVA prospects, it is possible to discover the companies that will experience unusual growth in their market value added (MVA). In this context, it should be no surprise to see that powerful wealth creators like Cisco Systems, Coca-Cola, and Microsoft Corporation have relatively high corpo-rate valuations because, in principle, *they should have*. This anticipation happens because the net present value of these high growth firms should track the explosive growth in their economic value added. Of course, the security selection "trick" is to avoid overpaying for the growth opportunities of wealth-enhancing firms.

Exhibit 1 provides some empirical insight on the EVA "growth style" of investing. This exhibit plots the profitability index ratio (ROC/COC) versus the value-to-capital ratio for the 50 largest U.S. wealth creators at year-end 1994.[4] Since the "value-cap" ratios in this exhibit are noticeably above unity, it is clear that wealth-enhancing companies have substantially *positive* MVA. At that time, high-growth firms like Coca-Cola and Cisco Systems were selling for multiples of 8.19 and 10.47 times the total capital employed in the respective businesses. In turn, the relatively high corporate valuations for these growth companies are sup-ported by profitability index ratios — 3.55 and 4.25, respectively — that are con-siderably higher than one. Not surprisingly, the favorable "residual return on capital" for growth companies like Coca-Cola and Cisco Systems is the underly-ing source of their seemingly high corporate valuations in the marketplace.

Oracle's positioning in Exhibit 1 makes for an interesting focal point to develop an EVA growth approach to active investing. In this exhibit, Oracle is dominated by wealth creators from both above and to the left of its position in real corporate profitability (ROC/COC) and relative-valuation space. With a "value-cap" ratio near 8, Coca-Cola's 3.55 profitability index ratio is considerably higher than the 2.40 figure observed for Oracle Corporation. Likewise, a look left-ward in Exhibit 1 reveals that Abbot Laboratories also dominates this high tech-

---

[4] The EVA-based data reported in this chapter was obtained for companies listed in the 1995 Performance 1000 Universe collected by Stern Stewart & Co.

nology company from a security selection perspective. For about the same level of real corporate profitability (ROC/COC near 2.4), Abbot's 3.75 value-to-capital ratio is dramatically lower than Oracle's 8.71 figure. Hence, for differing active reasons, Coca-Cola and Abbot Laboratories are the preferred investment choices.

From a *strict* security selection perspective, it is interesting to see that Coca-Cola dominates Microsoft Corporation. Coke's profitability index ratio is higher than the corresponding 3.31 figure observed for Microsoft, while this beverage firm's value-to-capital ratio is lower than the 9.2 figure for the rapidly-growing software services company. More importantly, Kellogg Company is clearly the preferred active choice over AirTouch Communications, Inc, as seen in Exhibit 1. For a similar relative valuation (near 3.85), the cereal company's 2.45 profitability index ratio is substantially higher than the dismal-looking 0.29 index figure for AirTouch Communications. Indeed, this communication's company's current valuation can only be sustained if investors are correct in their optimistic assessment of the firm's *future* ability to generate economic value added.

Based on their 1994 valuations, the exhibit also reveals that Philip Morris Companies and Intel are the preferred investment choices over Time Warner, Inc. Generalizing these modern security selection concepts reveals that the best investment opportunities include those companies with the highest EVA prospects (measured here by the profitability index ratio) for any given level of the value-to-capital ratio. Indeed, firms that plot on the *leftmost* portion of the "company cluster" shown in Exhibit 1 — Philip Morris, Intel, and Shering-Plough Corporation — as well as the high EVA growth companies — Coca-Cola, Cisco Systems and Microsoft — seem "actively efficient." Investing in these positive EVA companies appears to maximize the likelihood of financial success while minimizing the active risk of paying *too much* for the (debt and equity) securities of wealth-creating firms.

Exhibit 1: Profitability Index Ratio versus Value/Capital Ratio for 50 Largest U.S. Wealth Creators at Year End 1994

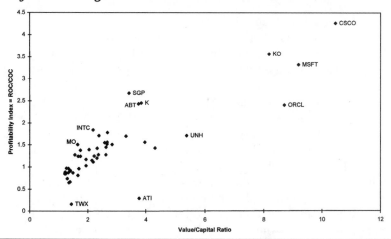

Exhibit 2: EVA Growth Strategy: Profitability Index Ratio: Actual versus Least-Squares Fitted for 1994

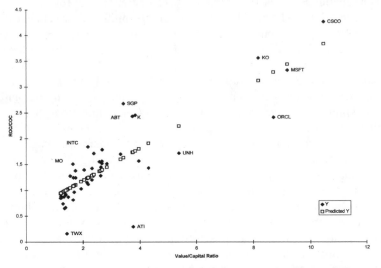

A Closer Look at the EVA Growth Strategy

It is also possible to use quantitative methods to identify the best growth opportunities in the marketplace. For instance, Exhibit 2 shows the actual versus *least-squares* fitted relationship between the profitability index ratio (ROC/COC) and the value-to-capital ratio for the 50 largest U.S. wealth creators at year-end 1994. The predicted PI ratios for these large capitalization firms were estimated according to:

$$PI = 0.56 + 0.31 \text{ [Value/Capital]}$$
$$\quad (5.73) \quad (11.09)$$

In this linear model, PI (dependent variable) is the ratio of the firm's after-tax return on capital (ROC) and the cost of capital (COC). The firm's economic value added is positive when the profitability index ratio is greater than unity, while its EVA is negative when the PI ratio is less than one. As expected, the "*t*-statistic" (shown in the parenthesis) on the value-to-capital factor (explanatory variable) for growth companies is highly significant.

Two points of reference are plotted in Exhibit 2 for each high growth company: (1) the actual profitability index ratio for a given level of the "value-cap" ratio, and (2) the predicted value of the PI ratio from the value/capital attributes in the linear regression model. In this exhibit, firms having profitability index ratios greater than those predicted by the regression model could then be viewed as attractive *buy* opportunities. Given their current valuation, their actual economic value added is greater than what was expected for similarly-valued growth companies. Conversely, growth firms with PI ratios that plot below the corresponding fitted values could then be placed on a *sell* or watch list, as their underlying EVA is too low in light of the relative valuation of their outstanding debt and equity securities.

In this context, Exhibit 2 shows why the high growth firms like Intel, Shering-Plough, Coca-Cola, and Cisco Systems were attractive buy opportunities at year-end 1994. In each case, their actual profitability index ratio is not only greater than unity (showing positive EVA for real growth companies), but also considerably greater than the fitted ratio that might normally apply for equally-valued growth companies in the marketplace. At 3.55 and 4.25, the profitability index ratios for Coca-Cola (the top U.S. wealth creator) and Cisco Systems were noticeably higher than their corresponding fitted values, 3.11 and 3.82. Likewise, Intel was an attractive buy opportunity at this time because its 1.84 profitability index ratio was 48% higher than the 1.24 index figure observed in the linear model.

The least squares model can also be used to identify the growth companies that were priced too high in light of their (current) EVA characteristics. Given their current valuations, Exhibit 2 shows that firms like Time Warner, Air Touch Communications, United Health Care, and Oracle Corporation had profitability index ratios substantially less than their corresponding fitted PI ratios. For instance, Time Warner's actual profitability index ratio at year-end 1994 was a paltry 0.16, while the fitted PI ratio was near unity, at 1.01. With a value-to-capital ratio of 1.44, the regression model suggests that this communications giant should have had a ROC that at least paralleled its COC. However, the firm's revealed PI ratio indicates that its after-tax capital return was 84% *below* the weighted average cost of capital. Thus, Time Warner Inc. was an unattractive investment opportunity at that time.

For similar pricing reasons, it is easy to see why the securities of Air Touch Communications, United Health Care, and Oracle Corporation (no less) were also relatively overvalued at year-end 1994. The revealed profitability index ratios for these growth-oriented companies were 0.29, 1.71, and 2.40, respectively. In sharp contrast, the fitted PI ratios for Air Touch Communications, United Health Care and Oracle were significantly higher at 1.73, 2.24, and 3.27. On balance, the quantitative analysis reveals that by focusing research efforts on growth companies having profitability index ratios that lie both below and above the fitted line, the active investor may see pricing trends that might otherwise go unnoticed in the marketplace. Moreover, because of possible credit rating changes, these corporate valuation considerations have joint pricing implications for the firm's outstanding equity *and* debt securities.

TOWARDS AN EVA VALUE STRATEGY

Since EVA emphasizes the importance of shareholder value, there is a natural tendency to associate this financial metric with the so-called "value style" of investing. After all, the traditional value model seeks to discover those firms with favorable earnings prospects that have fallen (unjustifiably so) out of favor with the consensus investor. Having said that, it is also important to recognize that the wealth-maximizing principles of modern corporate finance are applicable to all firms in the capital market, regardless of whether their investment fundamentals (growth rates, price-relatives, and dividend yield) would lead investors to categorize them as value- or growth-oriented companies.

By analogy, the EVA value approach to investing would largely emphasize the research importance of the "M," for market value added, in view of the "adjusted-E," for economic value-added. In this context, quality firms with value-to-capital ratios that lie below unity may have seen their security prices fall too far and too fast in view of the company's fundamental ability to generate positive net present value. By investing in the debt and equity securities of these presumably mispriced firms, the active investor seeks windfall gains on some, and possibly all, of the firm's outstanding securities. If correct, then the stocks of these "value-oriented" companies should rise in the market as the future reveals the better than market-assessed earnings prospects.

In light of the positive EVA announcements, the firm's outstanding debt securities may also rise in value due to unanticipated (from the general bond investor's viewpoint) "credit upgrades" in the junior and senior bonds. Of course, the opposite pricing implications would apply for the firm's outstanding debt and equity securities in the event that a deterioration occurs in its future ability to generate economic value added. Moreover, one of the major pricing features of this modern approach to corporate valuation is that fundamental changes in the firm's EVA may have information content for all of its securityholders.

Exhibit 3 sheds some interesting light on the 1994 "value characteristics" for the 50 largest U.S. wealth destroyers listed in the 1995 Performance 1000 Universe. Not surprisingly, this exhibit reveals that all 50 firms had a value-to-capital ratio that lies below unity. At that time, the market capitalization (including the value of the firm's outstanding bonds and stocks) figures for the so-called "wealth destroyers" were at a substantial discount from their aggregate "book capital." Knowledge of this overwhelmingly negative NPV finding for the bottom 50 U.S. companies is helpful, especially when attempting to develop a modern perspective on the "value approach" to active investing.

Exhibit 3 suggests that large wealth destroyers have relatively low corporate valuations because, in principle, *they should have*. These U.S. large capitalization firms have negative MVA because their revealed profitability index ratios (ROC/COC) are mostly less than unity. In this context, 45 of the 50 profitability index ratios for the companies shown in the exhibit are less than one. Hence, the economic source of the negative "net present value" finding for the 50 U.S. firms must in some sense be due to the low-returning (and therefore, negative EVA) capital investments that are being made by the corporate managers. On balance, these adverse investment decisions are the kind that investors feel will ultimately lead to after-tax capital returns that fall short of the weighted average cost of capital.

Exhibit 3: Profitability Index Ratio versus Value/Capital Ratio for 50 Largest U.S. Wealth Destroyers at Year End 1994

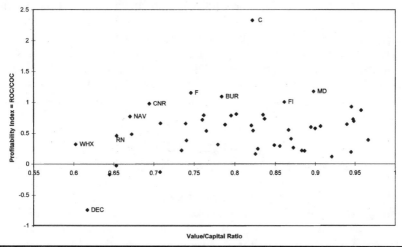

As with the traditional value approach to investing, the research challenge in the EVA model involves finding those companies having low corporate valuations in the presence of their positive earnings momentum. After all, buying the securities of firms with attractive earnings prospects at reasonable prices is what the value style of investing is really all about. This time, however, the real earnings factor can be measured either directly in terms of EVA or indirectly by looking at firms having a profitability index ratio (ROC/COC) that exceeds unity (for positive EVA). In this context, Exhibit 3 shows that only *five* firms pass the positive EVA (PI greater than one) and low corporate valuation ("value-cap" ratio less than unity) screen. At year-end 1994, these large capitalization companies included Ford Motor Company, Burlington Industries Equity, FINA, McDonnell Douglas, and Chrysler Corporation.

Although companies like Navistar International, RJR Nabisco Holdings, and WHX Corporation have positive profitability index ratios and notably low corporate valuations, their after-tax capital returns range from only 32% (WHX Corporation) to 77% (Navistar International) of their respective weighted average cost of capital figures. Hence, other things the same, their negative EVA excludes them from the active (value-oriented) opportunity set.

Among the five remaining candidates, Exhibit 3 shows that Chrysler Corporation was by far the best "value opportunity" at year-end 1994. This automobile company had the beneficial combination of a high profitability index ratio (ROC/COC = 2.33) in the presence of an aggregate corporate valuation (value-to-capital ratio = 0.82) that was 18% below the total "book capital" employed in the business. In other words, Chrysler was an exceptional value opportunity at that time because it had a comparatively low corporate valuation and an after-tax capital return that was 2.33 times the weighted average cost of its debt and equity capital.

Exhibit 3 also shows that Ford Motor Company was a better expected "value opportunity" than Burlington Industries Equity, McDonnell Douglas and FINA, Inc. With a profitability index ratio of 1.16, and a value-to-capital ratio of only 0.75, Ford Motor Company seems to "minimize" the active risk of paying too much for the shares of companies having similarly positive EVA — when measured relative to the book capital employed in the respective businesses. On the other hand, the exhibit reveals that Digital Equipment Corporation — with a 1994 after-tax capital return of –9.56% and a cost of capital of 12.87% — was also a value-oriented investment of sorts, but from a *shortselling* perspective!

DIVERSIFICATION AND
EFFICIENT MARKET CONSIDERATIONS

One of the limitations of any investment strategy (value or growth) that deviates from the "market portfolio" is that the resulting combination of securities may contain an excessive amount of active risk. This residual risk consideration is problematic for the value investor because in an informationally-efficient capital market there can only exist a small number of firms having both positive EVA momentum and low corporate valuations that haven't already been discovered in the marketplace. Unfortunately, this portfolio risk dilemma for the active investor doesn't necessarily go away by using quantitative techniques to identify the investable opportunity set of value-oriented companies.

For instance, Exhibit 4 shows the actual versus *least-squares* fitted relationship between the profitability index ratio (ROC/COC) and the value-to-capital ratio for the 50 largest U.S. wealth destroyers at year-end 1994. Like Exhibit 2, two points are displayed for each company, the actual profitability index ratio and the predicted PI ratio at that level of the value-to-capital ratio. In Exhibit 4, the fitted PI ratios for the bottom 50 firms in the 1995 Performance Universe were estimated according to:

$$PI = -0.33 + 1.09 \,[\text{Value/Capital}]$$
$$(-0.63) \quad (1.70)$$

The profitability index ratio is again obtained by dividing the firm' after-tax ROC by the weighted average COC. Unlike the t-statistic reported on the value-to-capital factor for the top 50 companies, the t-ratio for the set of value-oriented companies is statistically insignificant.

In order to understand the findings shown in Exhibit 4, it is helpful to recall that when the firm's profitability index ratio is equal to unity, its after-tax return on capital is just equal to the cost of capital. When this happens, the company's EVA is zero. This financial consideration is important because the two parameter estimates (intercept and slope) in the least squares model imply that the "value-cap" factor would have to equal 1.22 for the PI ratio to equal unity (thereby showing at least zero EVA for investors in these negative MVA firms).

However, the value-to-capital ratios for the last 50 U.S. firms in the Performance 1000 Universe were consistently below one.

In other words, the linear regression model predicted that the 50 largest wealth-destroyers in the 1995 Performance Universe would have negative economic value-added for 1994. As a result, the model offers no real basis for identifying the active set of value opportunities. Indeed, this empirical dearth of companies having both positive EVA and low corporate valuations (negative MVA) is a quantitative way of showing that "there really is no such thing as a free lunch." Real resources, in the form of time and money, will ultimately have to be expended to discover the best (ex-ante) security selection opportunities in the market.

A COMBINED LOOK AT THE EVA GROWTH AND VALUE CANDIDATES

Exhibit 5 shows the "top ten" security selections that might emerge from an EVA analysis of both growth *and* value companies. The eight growth-oriented firms — like Intel, Shering-Plough, Coca-Cola and Cisco Systems — were culled from Figure 2, while the two value-looking firms — Chrysler and Ford Motor Company — were selected from Exhibit 4 because of their attractive EVA/valuation characteristics. Among the 100 firms (50 top U.S. wealth creators and 50 largest wealth destroyers) covered in the research analyses, the ten large capitalization firms selected had both positive EVA momentum and comparatively low corporate valuations. This corporate valuation assessment was based on the statistical analyses of their profitability index ratios (ROC/COC) and the value-to-capital factor.

Exhibit 4: EVA Value Strategy: Profitability Index Ratio: Actual versus Least-Squares Fitted for 1994

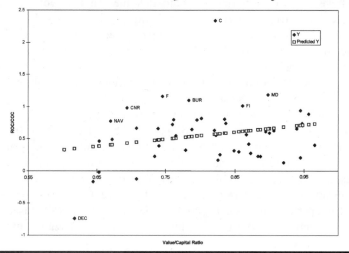

Exhibit 5: Top Ten Company Picks at Year-End 1994

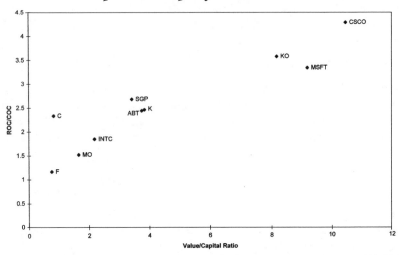

Not surprisingly, Chrysler Corporation stands out as one of the best investment opportunities at year-end 1994. With a value-to-capital ratio that was well below unity, this U.S. automaker had a profitability index ratio that paralleled the relatively higher-valued choices like Abbot Laboratories and Kellogg. Aside from Chrysler, though, Exhibit 5 shows a *positive* trade-off between the profitability index ratio and the value-to-capital measure for these U.S. large capitalization firms. Accordingly, this finding suggests that buying into companies with abnormally positive EVA characteristics — like Intel, Shering Plough, Coca-Cola, and Cisco Systems — comes at a higher price, as the more growth-oriented firms have noticeably higher corporate valuations.

However, it is important to note that the ten best companies in this exhibit were culled from two samples consisting of the top 50 and the bottom 50 firms listed in the Performance 1000 Universe at year-end 1994. For each company selected — ranging from Ford Motor with a relatively low corporate valuation, to Philip Morris and Intel with mid-level valuations, to Coca-Cola and Cisco Systems with high corporate valuations — the revealed profitability index ratio was considerably higher than the predicted PI ratio that would normally be associated with similarly-valued firms in the marketplace.

The active opportunity set can be expanded by selecting firms from a larger universe. This portfolio expansion would be beneficial for both performance and diversification reasons. Rather than looking at just the top 50 and the bottom 50 companies, the EVA analysis could be broadened to *discover* the best firms among all companies listed in the Performance 1000 Universe. On a larger scale it seems that substantial performance benefits could be derived from an EVA-based approach to company selection on both U.S. medium and small capitalization firms. Moreover, an international extension of the model might include an examination of the EVA/valuation characteristics of companies that operate in the developed foreign (MSCI-EAFE countries) and (IFC-based) emerging market regions of the world.

SUMMARY

This chapter looks at how EVA principles can be used to identify the best companies in the marketplace. In the growth strategy, the active investor seeks companies — due in large part to their exceptional product development and research capabilities — having an unusual ability to generate economic value added for the future. Based on the research analysis for 1994, it is no surprise to see that powerful wealth creators like Coca-Cola, Microsoft, and Cisco Systems fell into the high EVA-growth profile. By way of contrast, the modern value strategy emphasizes the security selection importance of firms with attractive EVA prospects that may have fallen mistakenly out of favor with the market's consensus investor. At that time, Chrysler Corporation — with exceptional EVA prospects and a low corporate valuation — was one of the best value opportunities among the large U.S. capitalization firms listed in the 1995 Performance Universe.

Although value and growth are often viewed as two distinct styles of investing, it is important to note that there are similarities between these active approaches to investment management. In each case, the active goal is to *maximize* the likelihood of financial success while *minimizing* the risk of paying too much for the shares of the evidently mispriced firms. In the EVA growth style, the investor tries to avoid paying excessive multiples for companies in the market that have unrealistic product development and earnings-growth expectations. In the EVA value strategy, the investor tries to avoid investing in the debt and equity securities of companies that may look "cheap" when, in essence, their seemingly low prices are an efficient market reflection of the firm's poor future growth opportunities. Indeed, at year-end 1994, this jointly negative EVA and MVA connection (due to a predominance of wealth wasters having profitability index ratios and value-to-capital ratios that were less than unity) is largely revealed for the bottom 50 firms in the Performance Universe.

It should also be emphasized that a correct assessment of whether a company is truly overvalued or undervalued needs to be based on an assessment of the firm's *future* ability to generate economic value added in view of its current valuation in the marketplace. Chrysler, for example, was considered a buy opportunity at year-end 1994 based on the presumption that its abnormally high EVA at that time was a positive signal about the firm's long-term ability to generate economic value added for the shareholders. On the other hand, if this automobile company were efficiently priced at year-end 1994, then investors would have been exceedingly pessimistic about the firm's future EVA capabilities in light of the currently favorable EVA announcement. This misestimation possibility is an unfortunate (from the active investor's perspective) yet integral component of active risk.

Finally, *real security analysis* involves a look beyond the numbers. In this context, it is helpful to remember that companies are manned by real people that produce real goods and services. This means that for any given earnings estimate (EVA-based or otherwise) to be realized, the firm needs to receive — within normal variation — the estimated number of orders that are consistent with the projected revenue growth rate, the product needs to be produced in a cost-efficient manner, and it needs to be packaged and delivered in a timely fashion to the customer. Bottlenecks along the way will impact the firm's realized performance results. Moreover, the firm's market value added (and therefore, its overall corporate valuation) is also shaped by forces that are beyond the control of its managers. These general forces include unanticipated shifts in consumer preferences, technological change within an industry, legal and regulatory rulings, and economy-wide and political changes.

Chapter 9

Industry Analysis Using EVA

At this point in time, there is a dearth of empirical research that focuses on the relationship between an industry's EVA and its underlying net present value. This empirical void is unfortunate because one of the basic tenets of a modern economy is that wealth is created when resources flow to their highest valued use. Fortunately, by using this innovative metric in an industry-based context, it may be possible to see those economic sectors that are creating wealth and those sectors that are not measuring up to their true wealth-enhancing potential.

Likewise, EVA analysis can be used to find industries that offer promising investment rewards. By focusing research efforts on economic sectors having attractive EVA prospects combined with reasonable valuations, it may be possible to form actively managed portfolios that outperform similar risk-indexed passive strategies. Moreover, since EVA emphasizes aggregate valuation, the methodology has sector-wide pricing and rating implications for both equities *and* bonds. In an attempt to shed some empirical light on these financial possibilities, let's first take a look at the wealth-creating features of some major U.S. industries.

FINANCIAL PREVIEW OF MAJOR U.S. INDUSTRIES

Exhibit 1 shows the financial characteristics of the top- and bottom-*five* U.S. industries listed in the 1995 Stern Stewart Performance Universe as ranked by their average market value added at year-end 1994. The upper portion of the exhibit reveals that the top three wealth-creating industries — beverages, personal care, and drugs and research — had positive average EVA in the presence of their favorable net present values. The EVA values ranged from $0.114 billion in the personal care and drugs and research industries up to $0.253 billion for the high-growth beverages sector. At that time, the average MVA values for the top three U.S. industries (measured in dollar terms) ranged from $4.569 billion for the drugs and research group, up to $9.465 billion for the beverages' industry.

This positive MVA and EVA association for the top three U.S. industries is due to their relatively high average return on capital in comparison with the weighted average cost of capital. With a profitability index ratio (ROC/COC) of 1.28, the after-tax return on capital for the drugs and research industry is 28% higher than the average capital cost for firms in this economic sector. Similarly, a look at the profitability index ratio for the typical beverage company reveals productive returns that exceed the weighted average cost of capital by 45%. On the other hand, the upper portion of Exhibit 1 also reports negative average EVA figures for the telephone and conglomerate industries at year-end 1994.

Exhibit 1: Top 5- and-Bottom 5 MVA-Ranked Industries in Performance Universe at Year-End 1994 (in U.S. $ Average Billions)

Section 1: Top 5 MVA-Ranked Industries

#	Industry	$MVA	$EVA	%ROC	%COC	PI*
1.	Beverages	$9.465	$0.253	14.744	10.138	1.45
2.	Personal Care	4.645	0.114	14.742	11.234	1.31
3.	Drugs and Research	4.569	0.114	15.932	12.409	1.28
4.	Telephone Comp.	4.196	−0.351	7.408	9.304	0.80
5.	Conglomerates	3.605	−0.019	11.301	11.609	0.97

* PI = Profitability Index Ratio (ROC/COC)

Section 2: Bottom 5 MVA-Ranked Industries

#	Industry	$MVA	$EVA	%ROC	%COC	PI*
52.	Aerospace	$0.253	−0.124	8.217	10.881	0.76
53.	Trucking and Ship.	0.249	−0.051	6.068	11.840	0.51
54.	Railroads	−0.030	−0.202	8.825	11.818	0.75
55.	Aluminum	−0.169	−0.452	3.440	11.510	0.30
56.	Cars and Trucks	−6.982	0.385	13.059	11.834	1.10

* PI = Profitability Index Ratio (ROC/COC)

At −$0.351 and −$0.019 billion, respectively, the negative EVA averages for the telephone and conglomerates sectors are interesting in light of their *contemporaneously* positive net present values. This industry pricing anomaly has at least two possible explanations. In particular, if the U.S. capital markets were largely efficient at that time, then investors must have been highly optimistic about the *future* earnings (EVA) prospects of companies operating within these economic sectors. If, in contrast, the financial markets were largely inefficient, then investors may have jointly mispriced (leading to overvaluation) the stocks and bonds of the average firm within the conglomerates and telephone industries.

With respect to the five lowest MVA-ranked industries at year-end 1994, the bottom portion of Exhibit 1 reports that these sectors had mostly negative average economic value added. Four industries in particular — ranging from aerospace (#52) down to aluminum (#55) — had consistently negative average EVA in the presence of their low positive to negative net present values. Indeed, the average after-tax return on capital (ROC) for the aluminum industry was only 30% (profitability index ratio at 0.3) of its 1994 average cost of capital, while the aerospace and railroad industries had average returns on productive capital of about 75% of their underlying cost of capital.

In sharp contrast, the cars and trucks industry (#56) stands out as a noticeable exception to the empirical finding that low positive- to negative-average MVA industries have typically negative average EVA values. At −$6.982 billion, the large negative average net present value figure for the automobile sector seems way out of line with its positive average EVA of $0.385 billion. With a profitability index ratio of 1.1, the average return on invested capital for the cars and trucks industry during 1994 was 10% higher than its average cost of debt and equity capital. As with the financial interpretations for the telephone and conglomerates industries, this anomalous pricing association between the MVA and EVA values for the automobile industry has (at least) two meaningful explanations.

One interpretation of the negative average MVA finding for cars and trucks is that investors may have grossly underestimated the long-term ability of this sector to generate economic value added. If correct, then the vehicle manufacturing firms that operate in this industry — spearheaded by the Chrysler Corporation — would have been an attractive "buy opportunity" for investors at year-end 1994. However, if the U.S. capital markets were generally efficient at that time, then the large negative average MVA figure for cars and trucks (−$6.982 billion) would indicate that investors were exceedingly pessimistic about the *future* EVA growth opportunities of the representative automobile firm.

TOWARDS A MODERN APPROACH TO INDUSTRY ANALYSIS

On a much broader scale, Exhibit 2 shows the MVA-to-capital and EVA-to-capital ratios for the 56 U.S. industries listed in the 1995 Performance Universe for year-end 1994. From an investment perspective, these size-adjusted financial measures can be used to identify those economic sectors that offered attractive EVA prospects for any given level of market value added. For instance, the exhibit shows that on average firms operating within the glass, metals, and plastic container industry were the better "buy opportunity" in comparison with companies that were operating in both the aluminum and steel industries. While the three industries have (somewhat) comparable MVA-to-capital ratios, the glass, metals, and plastic containers industry had positive EVA at a time when the EVA-to-capital ratios for the aluminum and steel industries were below −6%.

Exhibit 2 also shows that food retailing companies offered better investment prospects in relation to broadcasting companies at year-end 1994. For about the same MVA-to-capital ratio (near 0.5), food retailing had positive average EVA while broadcasting had negative. At that time, the average firm within the general manufacturing sector offered better EVA prospects than companies operating within the publishing sector. By extension, it appears that a modern-based approach to industry selection boils down to finding those sectors of the economy having *maximum* EVA prospects for any given level of industry valuation. This investment selection theme is consistent with the approach used to identify the best companies in the marketplace.

A closer look at Exhibit 2 reveals some attractive industry selection candidates at year-end 1994. In this context, the low yet positive EVA (and mostly "unfashionable") industries like cars and trucks; glass, metals, and plastic containers; food retailing; and, general manufacturing offered attractive earnings prospects for their relative sector valuations. In a similar manner, the high EVA-generating industries like business machines and services, semiconductors, beverages, and computer software and services had attractive earnings prospects for their noticeably higher industry valuations.

Taken together, these U.S. wealth-creating industries seem to describe an "efficient set" of active investment opportunities for 1994. For instance, Exhibit 2 shows that four economic sectors in particular — cars and trucks, general manufacturing, semiconductors, and computer software and services — occupy the *rightmost* position on the investable set of industry opportunities. At that time, these four sectors of the economy had the beneficial performance/risk characteristics of *maximum* EVA prospects for any given MVA-to-capital ratio and *minimum* industry valuations for their given levels of real corporate profitability.

It is also interesting to see in Exhibit 2 that the empirical relationship between the MVA- and EVA-to-capital ratios for U.S. industries looks non-linear. This possible non-linear relationship between the two measures of corporate success also seems present in the empirical findings for the 50 largest U.S. wealth creators and destroyers. Regression results reported earlier reveal that the EVA-to-capital ratio explains over 70% of the movement in the MVA-to-capital ratio for the top U.S. wealth creators, while the EVA factor explains little, if any, of the cross-sectional variation in the size-adjusted MVA for large U.S. wealth wasters. Moreover, with linearity and efficient capital markets, these findings may indicate that investors are overly optimistic about the EVA-generating abilities of growth industries like technology, while too pessimistic about the future earnings capabilities of the more value-oriented sectors of the economy.

Exhibit 2: MVA/Capital versus EVA/Capital Ratios: 56 U.S. Industries at Year End 1994

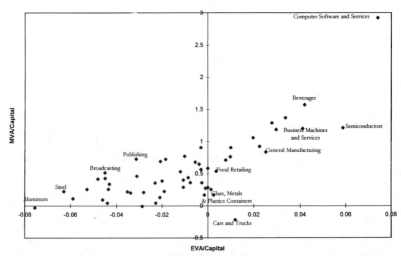

Exhibit 3: Profitability Index versus Value/Capital Ratio: 56 U.S. Industries at Year End 1994

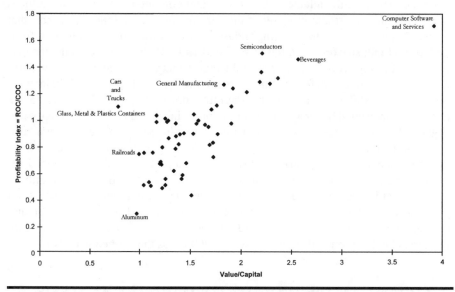

A CONVENTIONAL LOOK AT INDUSTRY ANALYSIS USING EVA

The benefits of using the EVA metric in an industry selection context can also be shown in a more conventional profitability versus relative valuation framework. Exhibit 3 shows a comparison of the profitability index (ROC/COC) ratio versus the value-to-capital ratio for the 56 U.S. industries listed in the Performance Universe at year-end 1994. The sector-wide pricing happenings in this exhibit are interesting in many financial respects.

Exhibit 3 indicates that the "cluster" of U.S. industries looks like the typical display of asset classes in a more conventional "asset allocation" approach to investment management. From an EVA perspective, the active goal is to invest in the equity *and* debt securities of those economic sectors having the highest profitability index ratio for any given level of industry valuation — measured this time by the value-to-capital ratio. Alternatively, the sector-allocation goal is determined by minimizing the value-to-capital ratio for a specified level of corporate financial success. In this way the active investor avoids paying *too much* for any given level of industry earnings, as determined by the spread between the sector's average return on capital and its overall average cost of capital.

The location of the "best industries" for active investing is clearly evident in Exhibit 3. Looking at industries having a profitability index ratio that exceeds one (for positive average EVA), one sees a variety of U.S. sectors that were attractively priced at year-end 1994. Given the performance results shown in Exhibit 2, it is no surprise to see that wealth-creating industries like cars and trucks, general manufacturing, semiconductors, beverages, and computer software and services were among the most attractive set of industry opportunities. Indeed, it seems that a portfolio of these wealth-creating industries would trace out an "efficient frontier" of real industry opportunities at year-end 1994. Diversification aside, the performance findings revealed in Exhibit 3 suggest that the cars and trucks industry was the best "active bet" for the future among the investable set of U.S. industries.

This exhibit also reveals that the railroad and aluminum industries have a relatively low valuation because their profitability index ratio is less than unity (for negative EVA). As a result, it seems that the active investor could construct a "two asset" portfolio consisting of securities in the glass, metal, and plastic containers and the cars and trucks industries that would offer a preferred trade-off of real average earnings for about the same relative valuation (near one). Better yet, Exhibit 3 suggests that it would have been possible to construct a "four industry" portfolio (at year-end 1994) consisting of cars and trucks, general manufacturing, semiconductors, and beverages that would have dominated the problematic multitude of U.S. industries having profitability index (ROC/COC) ratios that lie below unity.

QUANTITATIVE INSIGHTS ON INDUSTRY ANALYSIS USING EVA

In light of the exciting industry opportunities shown in Exhibit 3, let's now take a look at the information content of this performance graph from a more quantitative perspective. Three modeling approaches to describing the formal relationship between the profitability index ratio (ROC/COC) and the value-to-capital factor are presented here. These performance models include (1) a simple linear model, (2) a power model, or log-linear model, and (3) a "Markowitz-based" approach to modeling the relationship between the profitability index and value/cap ratios.

EVA Implications from a Simple Linear Model

The industry selection findings that were visually apparent in Exhibit 3 are also reinforced by the *linear* regression results shown in Exhibit 4. In particular, this exhibit displays the actual profitability index ratio versus the PI ratio that would be expected for the 56 U.S. industries at their relative industry valuations. The intercept and slope estimates for the sector-wide profitability index ratios at year-end 1994 were 0.223 and 0.438, respectively. The percentage of real industry earnings explained (adjusted R^2) by the value-to-capital factor is 57%, while the t-statistic, at 8.55, on the reported slope estimate is highly significant.

$$\text{PI} = \quad 0.223 + 0.438 \times \text{Value/Capital}$$
$$(t\text{-value}) \quad (2.66) \quad (8.55)$$

Exhibit 4: Actual PI Ratio versus Linear Fitted Ratios: 56 U.S. Industries at Year End 1994

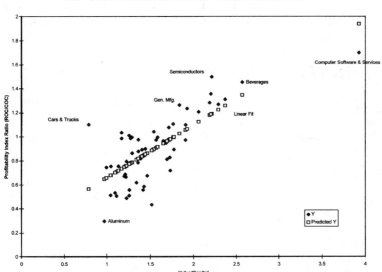

Exhibit 4 shows that the actual profitability index (ROC/COC) ratio for cars and trucks, general manufacturing, semiconductors and beverages industries were substantially higher than the corresponding "fitted values" from the linear model. At year-end 1994, the expected profitability index ratio for the cars and trucks industry was only 0.57, while the revealed PI ratio for the average automaker was 1.1 (for positive EVA). Likewise, the estimated (fitted) profitability index ratios for the semiconductor and beverages industries were 1.19 and 1.35, while the actual PI ratios for these high growth sectors of the economy were 1.5 and 1.45 respectively.

At the lower end of the valuation spectrum, Exhibit 4 shows that the 1994 profitability index ratio for the aluminum industry, at only 0.3, fell well below the 0.65 ratio that was expected for its given sector valuation. In effect, the actual EVA for this industry was below the negative EVA measure that was already expected for this traditional manufacturing sector. Additionally, if linearity is *supposed to* prevail in "real world" capital markets, then the simple regression model indicates that the computer software and services industry — at the high end of the valuation spectrum — was noticeably overvalued in the marketplace in view of its revealed (current) ability to generate EVA.

With a value-to-capital ratio of 3.92, the anticipated profitability index ratio (ROC/COC) for the computer software and services industry was 1.94. Although the actual profitability index ratio (1.7) for this high technology sector was the highest among the 56 U.S. industries covered in the research analysis, it fell short of the corresponding PI ratio that was predicted by the least squares model. That is, with linearity *and* efficient capital markets, this sector's valuation should have been more closely aligned with the relative valuations observed in the semiconductor and beverages industries. On the other hand, if real world capital markets are correctly described by nonlinear relationships in key financial variables — like the PI and "value-cap" ratios — then this high technology sector may have been priced "just right."

EVA Implications from a Log-Linear Model

Exhibit 5 expands the scope of the regression analysis by graphing the actual 1994 profitability index ratio versus the fitted PI values from both a simple linear model and a power, or log-linear, model. The latter model is used to capture some of the apparent "curvature" in the empirical relationship between the profitability index ratio and the value-to-capital factor shown in Exhibit 3, especially at the high end of the relative valuation spectrum. The regression coefficients in the log-linear model were estimated according to:

$$PI = a \, (\text{Value/Capital})^B$$
$$= 0.617 \, (\text{V/C})^{0.817}$$

where the coefficient "a," in log form, is the regression intercept, and B is the estimated sensitivity of the PI ratio to the (log) value-to-capital factor. The reported t-statistics on the estimated parameters were −8.03 and 6.62, respectively, while the adjusted R^2 value in the power (log-linear) model for 1994 was 43.79%.

Exhibit 5: Actual PI Ratio versus Log-Linear Fitted Ratios: 56 U.S. Industries at Year End 1994

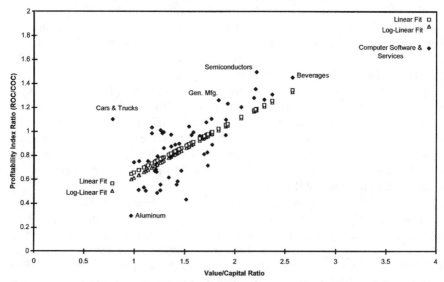

On the positive (forecasting) side, the log-linear model produces a better estimate of the actual profitability index ratio for the computer software and services industry in comparison with the simple linear model. At year-end 1994, the actual PI ratio for the computer software and services sector was 1.7, while the fitted value from the power model was 1.88. This compares favorably with the forecasted profitability index ratio, 1.94, for the computer software and services industry from the simple linear model. In effect, the log-linear model *has* captured some of the curvature that appears between the revealed PI ratios and the value-to-capital factor at the high end of the corporate valuation spectrum.

Exhibit 5 also reveals that at the lower end of the pricing spectrum, the curvature generated by the log-linear model produces a better estimate of the actual profitability index ratio for the aluminum industry when compared to the forecast ratio from the simple linear model. The actual 1994 PI ratio for this raw material sector of the economy was only 0.3, while the log-linear model produced a somewhat more optimistic PI ratio assessment of 0.6 (the linear fit for industry #55 was 0.65). Taken together though, the predicted 1994 EVA estimates for the aluminum industry from the two regression models were negative.

On the negative (forecasting) side, the percentage of PI variation explained for the 56 U.S. industries by the power model was lower than that observed in the simple linear model. The R^2 values in the two regression models for 1994 were 44% and 57%, respectively. As shown in Exhibit 5, the induced curvature in the fitted PI ratios from the log-linear model effectively decreases the forecast accuracy of the model for the high-growth EVA industries like semiconductors and beverages. From a comparative perspective, the model also reduces the predictability in the profitability index ratio for the attractive-looking cars and trucks sector, at the lower end of the relative valuation spectrum.

EVA Implications from the "Markowitz Model"

Some exciting EVA insights on industry analysis can also be obtained by describing the set of sector opportunities in the context of a two-asset Markowitz portfolio. If, for obvious reasons, one assumes that the "age of information technology" is here to stay, then investors might consider forming a "two-asset" portfolio consisting of a representative "market portfolio," along with an active "tilt" on the high-growth technology sector. For our purposes, the investment opportunities in the information technology sector can be characterized by the expected performance/risk features of the computer software and services industry. With these passive/active choices, the investor then chooses the "asset mix" that *maximizes* expected portfolio return for any perceived level of investment risk. In this scenario, conservative-minded investors might emphasize the "market portfolio," while pro-growth investors might place a high percentage of their portfolio funds in the information technology sector.

If we make the simplifying assumption that the *revealed* profitability index ratio (ROC/COC) is a measure (signal) of an asset's expected return, then the two-asset portfolio return can be described by:

$$E(R) = w_M \, E(R_M) + w_T \, E(R_T)$$
$$= w_M \, [PI_M] + w_T \, [PI_T]$$

where

$E(R)$ = the weighted average of the expected returns available on the two component assets in the portfolio

w_M = the proportion of portfolio funds invested in the so-called "market portfolio"

w_T = $(1-w_M)$ the portfolio weight assigned to the high-(EVA)growth technology sector.

The second $E(R)$ expression is written in terms of the profitability index ratios (PI) for the passive/active investment opportunities.

Upon substituting the profitability index ratios (at year-end 1994) for the Performance 1000 Universe and the computer software and services industry into the expected portfolio return equation, we obtain:[1]

$$E(R) = w_M \, [PI_M] + (1 - w_M) \, [PI_T]$$
$$= w_M \, [0.876] + (1 - w_M) \, [1.702]$$

where the expected return on the two asset portfolio is now described by the respective profitability index ratios and the proportion of portfolio funds invested in the representative market portfolio, w_M, and technology sector, $w_T = (1-w_M)$.

With a two asset portfolio, the expected risk can be captured with knowledge of (1) the investment weights, (2) the "own" volatility estimates — as measured by return standard deviation — and, (3) the correlation among the asset returns. In formal terms, the Markowitz risk equation for a two-asset portfolio can be expressed as:

$$SD(R) = \{ w_M^2 SD(R_M)^2 + w_T^2 SD(R_T)^2 + 2w_M w_T SD(R_M)SD(R_T)p(R_M,R_T) \}^{0.5}$$

In this portfolio risk expression the "SD" terms represent the return standard deviation figures, the "w" terms refer to the asset weights, and the $p(R_M,R_T)$ term measures the correlation among the market and technology sector returns.

If one also makes the simplifying assumption that the *actual* value-to-capital ratio is a measure of the "active risk" of paying too much for the shares of

---

[1] The PI ratio for the "market portfolio" is based on the capital-weighted profitability index ratio for 1994 that was available in the 1995 Performance Universe. Since Stern-Stewart revamped their weighing scheme in favor of market-value (MV) weights in their 1996 Performance Universe, this capital-based return series is no longer available.

However, since their "All-Simple Average" portfolio of 1000 companies had a 1994 profitability index ratio of 0.985 (still less than unity) and a value/capital ratio of 1.489 (close to the 1.451 figure used here) in the 1996 Performance Universe, the asset allocation issues with the alternative data would be similar to those presented in the text. Moreover, the quantitative linkage between the EVA and Markowitz models shown here is illustrative of how these innovative models can be used in practice.

wealth-enhancing firms, then the expected risk for the "two-asset" portfolio can be modeled directly in terms of the known "value-cap" ratios for the market portfolio and technology sectors, along with the estimated correlation between the EVA measures for these asset classes. Upon substituting the two "own volatility" estimates, at 1.451 and 3.923, respectively, and the (10-year) EVA correlation estimate, at 0.1806, into the portfolio risk equation, $SD(R)$, one then finds:

$$SD(R) = \{w_M{}^2[1.451]^2 + w_T{}^2[3.923]^2 + 2w_M w_T[1.451][3.923]0.1806\}^{0.5}$$

With this information it is possible to calculate the "plot points" for the two-asset Markowitz frontier, simply by varying the proportion of funds invested in the market portfolio, w_M (since $w_T = 1 - w_M$).

The resulting two-asset Markowitz curve is shown in Exhibit 6, in conjunction with the plot points for the 56 industry opportunities that were available for 1994. At the lower end of the curve, the "P1000" (for Performance 1000) point represents the return/risk combination for the passive "market portfolio," as measured empirically by the profitability index ratio for the Performance Universe at the revealed value/capital ratio of 1.451. In a similar manner, the highest expected return/risk point on the Markowitz curve consists of a 100% active investment in the information technology sector — as represented by the plot point in this exhibit for the computer software and services industry.

Among the findings in Exhibit 6, the two-asset curve reveals that the 85/15 combination lies at the lower end of the *positively* sloping portion of the Markowitz curve. This passive/active mix of the market portfolio and the information technology sector is interesting because a 100% allocation to the market portfolio alone results in a passive portfolio with negative EVA. This, in turn, suggests that a judicious mix of the market index (P1000) along with an active tilt toward technology produces a higher expected return for the same amount of risk. At the 85/15 mix, the portfolio has a profitability index ratio at precisely one (for zero EVA), while the market index at that risk level has negative EVA. That is, with a profitability index ratio of 0.876, the projected after-tax return on capital for the average firm in the 100% passive portfolio falls short of its average cost of capital.

Additionally, the Markowitz curve can be used to identify those industries that provided the best active opportunities (in retrospect) at year-end 1994. Cyclical industries like cars and trucks; glass, metal, and plastic containers; and general manufacturing that lie above the two-asset "efficient frontier" had better risk-adjusted performances than that available from the active/passive mix of the market index and the computer software and services sector. Likewise, at the higher end of the Markowitz curve, the semiconductor and beverages industries stand out (once again) as clear expected performance winners at year-end 1994. At that time, semiconductors had a profitability index ratio of 1.5, while the corresponding profitability index for the 50/50 mix of the market portfolio and high technology was 1.29.

Exhibit 6: Industry Selection using the Markowitz Model: 56 U.S. Industries at Year End 1994

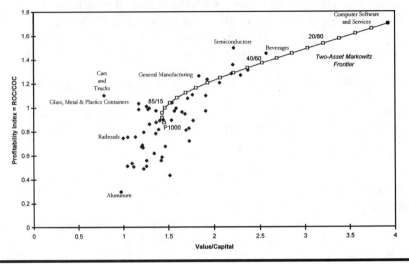

POSTSCRIPT ON WEALTH CREATION IN U.S. INDUSTRIES

A closer look at the financial components of EVA reveals the real source of wealth creation among U.S. industries. Exhibit 7 shows an interesting display of the average return on capital versus the average cost of capital for the 56 U.S. industries listed in the 1995 Performance Universe at year-end 1994. As expected, the exhibit reveals that wealth-creating industries have positive EVA because their after-tax return on capital exceeds the weighted average cost of capital. In contrast, economic sectors with low positive to negative net present value have adverse EVA because their average return on productive capital falls short of the average weighted cost of debt and equity capital.

Exhibit 7 reveals that the positive EVA-generating industries have capital returns that are substantially higher than the average cost of capital. The high EVA-growth industries like computer and software services, beverages, semiconductors, and business machines and services have after-tax capital returns that are considerably higher than their respective average cost of capital percentages. In turn, the average return on capital for the negative EVA-generating industries — publishing, broadcasting, steel, and aluminum — lie substantially below their average cost of capital figures.

Exhibit 7 also suggests that the source of the uncertainty in the EVA-to-capital ratio for U.S. industries is largely due to the volatility in the after-tax rate of return on capital. With a *cross-sectional* standard deviation of only 1.17%, the cost of capital among U.S. industries is noticeably stable around the economy-wide average capital cost of 11.15%. In contrast, at 3.84%, the standard deviation of the average after-tax capital return on U.S. industries is 3.28 times the industry-wide volatility estimate observed for the cost of capital factor. In a related manner, the 1994 after-tax return on capital for U.S. industries ranged from a low return of 3.44% in the aluminum industry up to a high average return of 22.4% for semiconductors.

These historical EVA comparisons highlight some of the difficult challenges that lie ahead for corporate managers and investors. Indeed, at 10.14%, the industry-wide average return on productive capital during 1994 was below the overall cost of capital of 11.15%. Moreover, Exhibit 7 shows that 37 of the 56 U.S. industries listed in the 1995 Performance Universe had average capital returns that fell short of the sector-wide average cost of debt and equity capital. These industry happenings are problematic for the entire U.S. economy.

SUMMARY

The benefits of using EVA analysis in an industry context are twofold. First, the MVA and EVA metrics provide a *direct* way of measuring the wealth impact of resource allocation in a free market economy. This powerful empirical recognition is perhaps most transparent when one looks at the positive net present values that are being generated in today's wealth-enhancing industries such as beverages, semiconductors, and computer software and services. These wealth findings contrast sharply with the unattractive MVA profiles of yesterday's industrial sectors such as aerospace, aluminum, and railroads. Indeed, EVA analysis can be used to capture the sector-wide NPV effects as economies evolve from agrarian to manufacturing powerhouses, on up the financial ladder to the present-day age of information technology — and beyond.

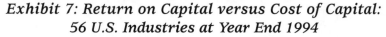

Exhibit 7: Return on Capital versus Cost of Capital: 56 U.S. Industries at Year End 1994

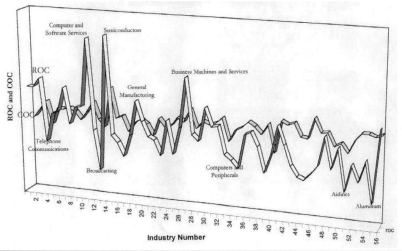

Second, EVA analysis can also be used as a screening tool to find those industries that offer attractive investment rewards. By focusing research efforts on those sectors having attractive EVA forecasts combined with reasonable valuations, it may be possible to form active strategies that outperform similar risk-passive portfolio strategies. Attractive industries that were reported at the low end of the valuation spectrum include sectors such as cars and trucks, general manufacturing, and glass, metals, and plastic containers. Likewise, powerful EVA-generating sectors, including semiconductors, beverages, and computer software and services, offer attractive return possibilities for the future even though their value-to-capital ratios are at the high end of the industry pricing spectrum.

Finally, it is important to emphasize that industry-based EVA analysis is still at its infancy. The preliminary findings reported in this chapter are encouraging in that some sectors of the economy — including beverages, semiconductors, and computer software and services — generate substantial value-added for their shareholders. However, the research analysis also demonstrates that many industries fail to live up to their true wealth-enhancing potential. This finding is supported by the fact that some 66% of the 56 industries examined at year-end 1994 had after-tax capital returns that fell short of their weighted average cost of capital. If correct, then this negative average EVA finding for U.S. industries may be symptomatic of underlying structural problems for the general economy.

Chapter 10

Macro-Analysis Using EVA

EVA offers some special insights into the source of wealth creation at the macro-economic level. When the economy-wide return on capital is higher than the cost of capital, then a nation's economic value added is positive. In principle, this favorable residual capital return situation should lead to positive net present value (MVA) for the entire economy. In contrast, if the country-wide capital return falls short of the average cost of capital, then the national EVA will be negative — even though the overall return on capital (ROC) may be greater than the general level of interest rates.

If this economic malaise persists, then the ensuing national decline in wealth will lower the country's overall standard of living. In effect, these powerful EVA predictions suggest that a nation's financial wealth hinges on the balance between two macro-economic drivers — in particular, the after-tax return on productive capital and the economy-wide cost of capital. Equivalently, the real test of whether a nation's wealth level is increasing or decreasing is the *sign* of the country's residual (or surplus) return on capital. On balance, a positive RROC is wealth-increasing, while a negative residual capital return that persists will ultimately destroy a nation's wealth.

While the primary responsibility for creating shareholder wealth lies on the firm's managers, the general economic climate can impact the firm's ease or difficulty in meeting its fiduciary duties to the shareholders. Fiscal policy steps at the macro-level that are designed to *permanently* lower taxes, decrease business regulation, and spur capital formation (for example, investment tax credits for physical and human capital) make it easier for firms to collectively increase the level of national wealth. On the other hand, adverse fiscal policy decisions that lead to higher personal and corporate taxes, non-productive governmental spending, more business red-tape, and investment disincentives ultimately impede the wealth-creating opportunities of firms that are operating in the real economy.

Additionally, monetary policy actions can either support or hinder the wealth-enhancing efforts of companies operating at the micro level. On the positive side, central banks can support the EVA-generating efforts of firms by taking monetary steps that keep inflation in check and, therefore, interest rates at favorable levels for business expansion. As interest rates fall in the economy, the NPV of firms rises as the EVA streams of otherwise unacceptable projects now look acceptable. Also, responsible central bank actions that seek to enhance investor confidence in the economic stability of a nation can have a *doubly* beneficial effect on the economy-wide cost of capital. This happens when the wealth-enhancing decline in the "risk-free interest rate" is reinforced by a fall in the capital market's risk premium for bearing national business risk.

Exhibit 1: U.S. Capital Returns and Capital Costs during the 1984 to 1995 Period

Year	Return on Capital (ROC%)	Cost of Capital (COC%)	Residual Return on Capital (RROC%)
1984	14.89	15.73	-0.84
1985	13.40	14.34	-0.94
1986	12.21	11.69	0.52
1987	13.13	12.69	0.44
1988	13.06	13.29	-0.23
1989	12.24	12.99	-0.75
1990	11.46	13.06	-1.60
1991	10.13	12.69	-2.56
1992	10.67	12.39	-1.72
1993	10.71	11.69	-0.98
1994	12.19	12.37	-0.18
1995	13.05	11.60	1.45
Average	12.26	12.88	-0.62
Standard Deviation	1.36	1.19	1.10

THE MACRO-ECONOMIC ROLE OF EVA: INTRODUCTION

Knowledge of the major EVA drivers can be used to make some interesting inferences about the strength of the economy, as well as the general movement of security prices. In this context, Exhibit 1 presents a listing of the U.S. return on capital, the economy-wide cost of capital, and the U.S. "residual return on capital" for the twelve year period from 1984 to 1995.[1] From a time series perspective, the exhibit shows that the overall U.S. average return on capital during the reporting period fell short of the average cost of capital. At 12.26%, the time-weighted U.S. capital return was 62 basis points below the average economy-wide cost of capital.

In view of this pervasive negative EVA finding, it is encouraging to see that three of the reporting years had cross-sectional average capital returns that were higher than the economy-wide cost of capital. At 0.52% and 0.44%, the U.S. residual return on capital (RROC) was positive in 1986 and 1987, respectively. However, after spiraling *downward* in the post-1987 years, Exhibit 1 reveals that it was not until 1995 that the U.S. economy again posted an after-tax capital return that exceeded the national cost of capital.

---

[1] The EVA-based figures — such as the economy-wide return on capital and the average cost of capital — reported in this chapter are largely based on the "All-Simple Average" series listed in the 1996 Performance 1000 Universe. These all-simple averages cover 1987 to 1995, while the 1995 Performance Universe was used to obtain the economy-wide simple averages for the 1984 to 1986 period.

Exhibit 2: Average U.S. Return on Capital versus Cost of Capital: 1984 to 1995

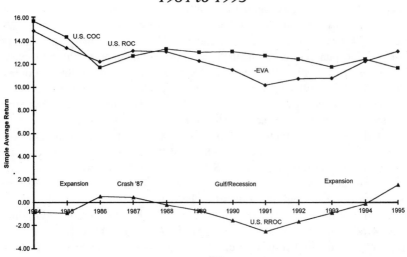

During these problematic years, the return on capital was somewhat more volatile than the economy-wide cost of capital. This observation is based on the 1.36% standard deviation calculated on the U.S. capital return series reported in Exhibit 1. This ROC- volatility estimate is somewhat higher than the comparable uncertainty figure, 1.19%, for the economy-wide cost of capital.

A CLOSER LOOK AT THE U.S. REAL ECONOMY

Exhibit 2 provides a graphical display of the U.S. return on capital, the economy-wide cost of capital, and the U.S. residual return on capital for the 1984 to 1995 period. For discussion purposes, the exhibit can be examined in terms of four seemingly unique time periods according to varying EVA patterns in the U.S. economy. The representative subperiods (presented below) can also be used to demonstrate the power of the two-factor EVA model — with an emphasis on the economy-wide *spread* between the average return on productive capital and the cost of capital — versus a single-factor ROC (or, COC) model.

EVA Phase I: Falling ROC and Falling COC

Subperiod I consists of the three years spanning 1984 to 1986. This time period is interesting from an EVA perspective because the U.S. after-tax return on capital was falling in the presence of a *rising* residual return on capital. At that time, the economy-wide cost of capital was decelerating — due to a sharp decline in Treasury bond yields — at a faster rate than the observed decline in the U.S. after-tax capital return. For instance, at year-end 1984, the U.S. cost of capital was at an excessively-high rate of 15.73%. By the end of 1986, the economy-wide capital cost had declined 404 basis points to 11.69%.

In contrast, Exhibit 2 shows that the U.S. return on capital fell from 14.89% at year-end 1984 down to 12.21% at year-end 1986. This represents a 268 basis point decline in U.S. capital returns during the two-year reporting interval. Taken together, the exhibit shows that the *spread* between the U.S. return on capital and the cost of capital rose from –0.84% for 1984, up to 0.52% in December 1986. This fundamental improvement in the U.S. economy is captured in an EVA context by the upward-sloping pattern of the residual return on capital series in the three years spanning 1984 to 1986.

Indeed, the two-factor EVA model — as reflected in the passing of the U.S. residual capital return series from negative to positive — shows that the wealth-enhancing potential of the U.S. economy was actually improving, even though a one-factor return on capital focus would suggest otherwise. Moreover, this crossing-point of negative to positive EVA for the economy is also captured by the cutting of the U.S. COC function from *below* by the average return on capital. Knowledge of this powerful crossing point — as also reflected in the yearly behavior of the residual return on capital series — is the foundation for understanding the source of economic growth and "the wealth of nations."

EVA Phase II: Downward Turning ROC with Rising COC

Subperiod II focuses on the EVA happenings during the two-year period covering 1987 and 1988. This time period is interesting because it shows that the U.S. ROC actually "peaked" in the same year that the U.S. stock market experienced Black Monday, October 19, 1987. During this year of heightened uncertainty, Exhibit 2 shows that the U.S. COC was rising at a faster rate than the economy-wide ROC. At 13.13% in 1987, the U.S. return on capital was only 44 basis points above the economy-wide cost of capital. Then, in 1988, the U.S. ROC was falling while the national cost of capital was still rising.

Likewise, Exhibit 2 reveals that at year-end 1986, the U.S. residual return on capital was at the turning point of what ultimately became an unprecedented decline in economic value added for the economy. For 1987, the U.S. RROC was 0.44%, while at year-end 1988 the U.S. surplus return on capital was –0.23%. Hence, the two-factor EVA model reveals that the real economy peaked at year-end 1986 and then began its substantial downward decay when the residual capital return series was moving from positive to negative. This means that during 1988 the economy's EVA turned negative when the U.S. COC was cut from *above* by the downward spiraling ROC series.

Additionally, the 1986 to 1987 turning behavior in the U.S. residual return on capital is especially interesting in light of the efficient-versus-irrational markets' interpretations of the October Crash of 1987.[2] For obvious reasons, it has been difficult for the efficient markets' proponents to argue that the U.S. stock

---

[2] The finance literature abounds with interesting research on the events surrounding Black Monday, October 1987. For this author's interpretation see James L. Grant, "Stock Return Volatility during the Crash of 1987," *Journal of Portfolio Management* (Winter 1990).

market was efficient in the sense of reflecting "full information" at the time of the crash. In the absence of any surprise negative information that might actually spark such an event, what therefore was the point of the 20% decline in U.S. security prices on Black Monday, October 19, 1987? As a result, behaviorists — with their convenient, yet unsubstantiated, claims of market "bubbles" — have seized the explanatory moment of the day.[3]

Despite the irrational-based characterizations of the October 1987 market break, the EVA evidence is consistent with a more fundamental economic view of this adverse financial event. In this context, Exhibit 2 reveals that it is plausible that the October Crash of 1987 occurred because investors perceived that a powerful negative change was about to impede the U.S. economy's ability to generate economic value added for the future. If correct, then security prices should have fallen dramatically when investors perceived that the forthcoming negative EVA happenings at the macro level would ultimately destroy wealth.

The emerging benefits of looking at the real economy from an EVA perspective should now be transparent. During EVA phase I, a single-factor emphasis on a traditional profitability measure like ROC would have led to an incorrect assessment of the future direction of the U.S. economy. Likewise, a one-factor focus on interest rate happenings in the U.S. Treasury bond market (an integral component of COC) during 1987 and 1988 would have led to an incomplete assessment of the financial health of the real economy. Indeed, the sharply *falling* spread between the U.S. return on capital and the cost of capital during these two years is a powerful justification for jointly utilizing the information content of the two-factor (ROC and COC) EVA model.

EVA Phase III: Falling ROC with Neutral COC

Subperiod III focuses on the balance between the U.S. return on capital and the cost of capital during the 1989 to 1991 years. This three-year period is characterized by economic malaise due to the sharp decline in the U.S. after-tax return on capital in the presence of mostly stable interest rates. At year-end 1989, the U.S. after-tax return on capital was 12.24%. By 1991, the economy-wide capital return had declined 211 basis points to 10.13% Meanwhile, the marginal decline of 30 basis points in the U.S. cost of capital during these troubling years offered no assistance whatsoever in helping to prevent the "free-fall" in the national EVA, and therefore, the general well-being of the U.S. economy.

Taken together, these ROC and COC patterns (Exhibit 2) led to the "bottoming out" in the U.S. residual return on capital series during 1991. For that dismal-looking year, the U.S. residual return on capital was −2.56%, the lowest point in the RROC series for the 12-year period covered in the research analysis. On balance, the EVA model indicates that a powerful recession was underway during 1990

---

[3] For a market "bubble" interpretation of the October 1987 stock market break, see Robert J. Shiller, "Who's Minding the Store?," *The Report of the Twentieth Century Fund Task Force on Market Speculation and Corporate Governance* (New York: The Twentieth Century Fund Press 1992).

and 1991. Moreover, the two-factor model shows that the source of the recession in 1990 and 1991 was mostly due to the sharp decline in the U.S. return on capital in the presence of an interest rate environment that largely remained unchanged.

Additionally, the EVA findings in the 1989-1991 subperiod contrast with the empirical findings reported in the first subperiod (1984-1986) where ROC was falling, but at a much slower rate than the U.S. COC. Thus, the economy-wide EVA behavior (positive in the earlier years, versus negative more recently) is noticeably different for the two phases of the U.S. economy, even though the average return on capital was decelerating in both instances.

EVA Phase IV: Rising ROC and Falling COC

Subperiod IV shows the time series behavior of the U.S. return on capital and cost of capital from 1992 to 1995. This four-year EVA phase is particularly interesting because the U.S. after-tax return on capital was rising sharply at a time when the economy-wide cost of capital was mostly falling. At year-end 1991, the U.S. return on capital was 10.13%, while in December 1995 this traditional profitability measure had risen to 13.05%. During this economic growth period, the U.S. cost of capital fell from 12.69% at year-end 1991 to 11.6% four years later.

This powerful EVA growth phase — with its inception clearly traced back to 1991 — continued into 1995 as the economy was still quite robust and U.S. Treasury bond yields dropped 200 basis points since December 1994. Moreover, the powerful recovery in the U.S. economy in recent times is also revealed in Exhibit 2 by the sharply rising U.S. residual return on capital series in the post-1991 years. At year-end 1991 the U.S. RROC was −2.56%, whereas at year-end 1995 this "surplus return on capital" had just turned positive at 1.45%.

1995 was also the first year in recent times that the U.S. residual return on capital was positive since it peaked, at 0.52%, in 1986. Indeed, the upward-sloping behavior of the residual capital return series in 1995 is entirely consistent with an efficient market's explanation of the seemingly explosive growth in the U.S. capital market. Indeed, this empirical interpretation of the recent growth in the U.S. stock *and* bond markets contrasts sharply with Fed-Chairman Alan Greenspan's conjecture of "irrational exuberance" by investors and a fundamental separation between the U.S. real economy and the financial happenings in the capital markets.

INTEREST RATE DEVELOPMENTS AND THE TWO-FACTOR EVA MODEL

Exhibit 3 presents an interesting time series display of the U.S. return on capital, long-term treasury bond yields, and the U.S. residual return on capital from 1984 to 1995. Among other things, this exhibit can be used to show the power of the two-factor EVA model over a single-factor interest rate model.[4]

---

[4] Long-term government bond yields shown in Exhibit 3 were obtained from Ibbotson Associates, *Stocks, Bonds, Bills and Inflation — 1996 Yearbook* (Chicago: Ibbotson Associates, 1996).

Exhibit 3: U.S. Capital Returns, Treasury Yields, and the Residual Return on Capital: 1984 to 1995

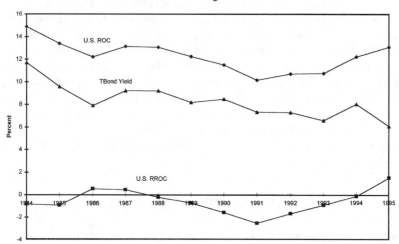

In particular, the exhibit shows that while the yearly U.S. after-tax return on capital was greater than the corresponding (pre-tax) Treasury bond yield during the 1984 to 1995 period, the U.S. residual return on capital was only positive for three of the 12 reporting years. This implies that knowledge of the inflation (and therefore, interest rate) happenings in the Treasury bond market are a necessary, but insufficient, condition for understanding how wealth is truly created in a well-functioning capital market.

To illustrate this point, consider the post-1987 behavior of the U.S. cost of capital in Exhibit 2 in the context of the interest rate happenings revealed in Exhibit 3. In the former exhibit, the U.S. capital cost was largely falling because Treasury bond yields, as shown in Exhibit 3, were generally declining in these post-crash years. However, the two-factor EVA model — with its joint focus on the relationship between after-tax capital returns *and* capital costs — shows that the economy-wide EVA was sharply falling. In turn, this adverse RROC development in the post-1987 years occurred because the economy-wide return on capital was falling at a *faster* rate than the general decline in interest rates.

Other things remaining the same, a decline in interest rates should lead to an improvement in both the country-wide EVA and the national wealth level. For better or worse, Exhibit 3 shows that interest rate changes rarely occur in a vacuum. Moreover, while interest rates "spiked up" in 1994 (due, in my view, to harsh interest rate actions taken by the Fed), the economy-wide EVA went up. Surely, the national EVA didn't go up because investors thought that higher Treasury bond yields were somehow good for the economy. Rather, the economy-wide EVA rose in 1994 because the U.S. after-tax return on capital was rising at a *faster* rate than the U.S. cost of capital.

This EVA focus on the after-tax return on capital should not be taken to mean that a single-factor ROC focus will lead to more meaningful insights about the direction of a nation's EVA or its national wealth level in comparison with a one-factor emphasis on COC. Indeed, Exhibit 3 shows the U.S. residual return on capital was rising during 1985 and 1986 at a time when the U.S. after-tax return on capital was actually falling. This positive EVA development occurred at that time because the U.S. cost of capital (led by declining Treasury bond yields) was declining at a faster rate than the overall fall in the U.S. return on capital.

Taken together, Exhibits 2 and 3 *do* suggest that the "real key to creating wealth" for a nation lies in a keen understanding of the economic prominence of the residual (or surplus) return on capital. This knowledge is in turn derived from a joint appreciation of the economic relationships between the after-tax capital return and economy-wide cost of capital.

EVA IMPLICATIONS BY PRESIDENTIAL YEARS

The macro-EVA data can also be used to assess the strength of the U.S. economy during recent Presidential years. Although the positive or negative wealth conse-quences observed here do *not* necessarily mean that they were caused by the par-ticular party in office — either a Democratic or Republican President — the historical possibilities are interesting to explore just the same. In this context, Exhibit 4 presents a time series plot of the U.S. after-tax return on capital, the economy-wide cost of capital, and the U.S. residual return on capital for five of the eight Reagan Years (1984 to 1988), the Bush Years (1989 to 1992), and three of the current Clinton Years (1993 to 1995).

Exhibit 4: Average U.S. Return on Capital versus Cost of Capital: Recent Presidential Years

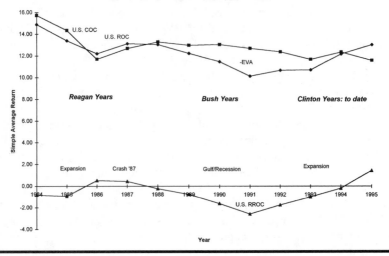

The Reagan Years

The Reagan Years span the first and second EVA phases that were examined in the context of Exhibit 2. During the first five reporting years (or the last five years Ronald Reagan was president) the U.S. residual return on capital rose considerably from 1985 to 1986, and then declined substantially during 1988 when the RROC series turned negative. On balance, Exhibit 4 shows that the reported Reagan years were largely EVA-increasing (although not necessarily associated with positive EVA) because the after-tax return on capital was moving in a direction that eventually (in 1986) cut the U.S. cost of capital series from *below*.

This initial narrowing of the ROC and COC spread during the reported Reagan years was the precondition for the positive residual return on capital (and therefore, EVA) generated by the U.S. economy during 1986 and 1987. However, the subsequent cutting of the economy-wide cost of capital series from *above* by the U.S. return on capital during 1988 was a powerful precondition for impending economic and financial malaise — whereby, some of the anticipatory adverse wealth effects were possibly "priced" on Black Monday as part of the capital market's unprecedented negative EVA-outlook for 1988 and beyond.

The Bush Years

Although the Reagan years seem mostly EVA-increasing, the first three years of the Bush presidency were EVA-decreasing. Indeed, the Bush tenure is largely coincident with EVA phase III (1989 to 1991), where ROC was rapidly decelerating in the presence of a relatively flat cost of capital series. At −2.56% in 1991, the U.S. residual return on capital reached its lowest point in the 12-year reporting period shown in Exhibit 4. At that time the U.S. cost of capital was 12.69%, while the after-tax return on productive capital was 10.13%.

After "bottoming-out" in the third year of the Bush Presidency, it is interesting to see that the U.S. residual return on capital was on the road to recovery in 1992. That EVA was increasing in the final year of the Bush Administration is easily identified in Exhibit 4 by either (1) the upward turn in the RROC series, or equivalently, (2) the rise in the U.S. after-tax capital return during 1992, in the presence of the falling cost of capital. In effect, the free-fall in EVA — that evidently dates back as far as 1987 — finally began its positive turnaround at year-end 1991. Therefore, the EVA evidence strongly indicates that the current U.S. recovery began in the last year of the Bush Presidency.

The Clinton Years

Although some might still quarrel about the exact turning point in the latest economic recovery, Exhibit 4 shows that the Clinton Years to date have been associated with a period of sharply rising EVA. Indeed, from 1993 to 1995 the U.S. after-tax return on capital was rising in the presence of a (mostly) falling cost of capital. When in 1994 the U.S. ROC series approached the U.S. COC series from *below*, this EVA-happening set the stage for the large positive residual capital return that finally occurred in 1995. At year-end 1994, the exhibit also shows that the U.S. residual return on capital series (and therefore, the economy-wide EVA) passed through *zero* with an upward-sloping vengeance for 1995.

As with many of the Reagan years, the Clinton years have been associated with both rising and (sometimes) positive EVA. A comparative inspection of the two-factor EVA model shows that the U.S. residual return on capital was largely rising during the reported Reagan years because of a sharp decline in the U.S. cost of capital from 1984 to 1986. The U.S. capital cost declined in these years because of the favorable news conveyed by falling Treasury bond yields and, possibly, a decline in the market's assessed premium for bearing national business risk. In turn, the Clinton Administration has presided over an economy with sharply rising business returns in the presence of a comparatively smaller decline in the U.S. cost of capital.

Although the economic and political circumstances may differ by Presidential years, the EVA recoveries that happened during the Reagan and Clinton years were signaled by the crossing of the COC series from *below* by the economy-wide return on capital. Moreover, when the ROC series is rising at a time when the COC is falling, this, in principle, sets the stage for a powerful upward movement in *both* bond and stock prices. Indeed, the explosive growth in the U.S. stock and bonds markets during 1995 seems consistent with the efficient market predictions of the two-factor EVA model.[5]

SUMMARY

This chapter focuses on the benefits of using EVA in assessing the underlying strength of the economy. With its two-factor emphasis on balancing the after-tax return on capital *and* the economy-wide cost of capital, the model offers some major economic and financial insights. In particular, when the after-tax capital return exceeds the economy-wide cost of capital, then a nation's EVA is positive. In principle, this positive residual (or surplus) return on capital situation is a powerful precondition for wealth creation at the country level.

Additionally, the EVA model suggests that a nation's net present value should be rising in the presence of an expansion in the *spread* between the economy-wide return on capital and the average (of the weighted-average) cost of debt and equity capital. In contrast, the national NPV decelerates, in theory, when the residual return on capital (for varying ROC and COC reasons) is falling. These are both powerful *and* testable macro-economic implications of the two-factor EVA model.

The economy-wide empirical evidence is important in many respects. From 1984 to 1995, the U.S. residual return on capital was mostly negative. This

---

[5] For an examination of the role of historical return and risk estimates in predicting stock prices in recent years, see James L. Grant, "Forecasting Stock Prices in the Post-Crash Era," *Journal of Investing* (Special Technology Issue: Winter 1995).

adverse EVA happening is not unique to any particular political party as the national EVA was negative (but improving) at times in both the Reagan Years and the Clinton Years (to date). Indeed, the fact that the U.S. economy had a positive residual return on capital during 1986 and 1987, and then the RROC series turned substantially negative until 1995 is indicative of a fundamental imbalance between the U.S. return on capital and the economy-wide cost of capital.

However, since U.S. interest rates were largely falling in the post-(1987) crash years, the source of the negative EVA happening for the general economy seems to be a productivity issue — and possibly a business and capital gains taxation issue — that manifests itself in a relatively low U.S. after-tax return on capital. In fact, the national EVA finally took a historic turn in 1991 when the economy-wide return on capital "bottomed-out" in the presence of a falling U.S. cost of capital.

Finally, macro-EVA analysis offers a powerful research synergy for those financial institutions that are traditionally separated along bond and equity market lines of research. By jointly focusing research efforts on the positioning of the return on capital relative to the cost of capital, both "Fed watchers" and equity strategists alike may see powerful economic and financial trends that might otherwise go unnoticed in a more conventional realm of financial analysis. In essence, EVA brings these seemingly unrelated bond and equity research groups back to a financial place called "home."

INDEX

121